Play The Forest School Way

Woodland Games, Crafts And Skills For Adventurous Kids

Peter Houghton
Jane Worroll

16pt

Copyright Page from the Original Book

Play the Forest School Way
Peter Houghton and Jane Worroll

First published in the UK and USA in 2016 by
Watkins, an imprint of Watkins Media Limited
19 Cecil Court
London WC2N 4EZ

enquiries@watkinspublishing.co.uk

Copyright © Watkins Media Limited 2016
Text copyright © Peter Houghton and Jane Worroll 2016
Artwork copyright © Peter Houghton and Jane Worroll 2016

The right of Peter Houghton and Jane Worroll to be identified as the Authors of this text has been asserted in accordance with the Copyright, Designs and Patents Act of 1988.

All rights reserved. No part of this book may be reproduced in any form or by any electronic or mechanical means, including information storage and retrieval systems, without permission in writing from the publisher, except by a reviewer who may quote brief passages in a review.

Development Editor: Fiona Robertson
Head of Design: Viki Ottewill
Designer: Manisha Patel
Production: Uzma Taj
Commissioned artwork: Peter Houghton

A CIP record for this book is available from the British Library

ISBN: 978-1-78028-929-8

10 9 8 7 6 5 4 3 2 1

Typeset in Archer
Colour reproduction by XY Digital
Printed in Slovenia

www.watkinspublishing.com

PUBLISHER'S NOTE:
Some activities in this book, for example those involving fire or cutting tools, may be dangerous if instructions are not followed precisely. Always follow manufacturers' instructions when using tools. Wild foods such as berries can be poisonous, so eat only what you can identify as safe. Adults need to assess each child's capabilities and supervise any potentially dangerous activity at all times. Watkins Media Limited, or any other persons who have been involved in working on this publication, cannot accept responsibility for any injury, illness or damages that result from participating in the activities in this book.

TABLE OF CONTENTS

Introduction	i
Nature Explorers	1
JOURNEY STICK	3
WOODLAND MAPPING	10
ACORN HIDE-AND-SEEK	16
SCAVENGER HUNT	22
MY TREE	28
PHOTOGRAPHIC MEMORY	34
Forest Arts	41
MAGIC WANDS	43
MUD FACES	50
NATURE'S HEADDRESSES	57
ICE ART	63
BOW AND ARROW	72
WOODLAND JEWELLERY	82
STICK FRAMES	100
Survival Skills	108
ESSENTIAL KNOTS	110
BUILDING SHELTERS	126
MAKING FIRE	142
CHIMNEY KETTLE	152
WILD FOOD	161
Wildlife Team Games	177
WHAT'S MY ANIMAL?	179
FOREST FIRE	185
PREDATORS TRACK PREY	191
WEB OF LIFE	199
BAT AND MOTH	206
HUNGRY BIRDS	213

ANT TRAIL   220
SLEEPING BEAR   226

Introduction

Nature offers us a sanctuary, a place where we can find peace and wonder. It is not limited by time or confined by walls, and even today we cannot control it completely. It is much larger and older than we are, and its rhythms resonate deep within us. Nature is where we are from and where we belong, and our survival is intricately linked to its existence. For children it is the greatest playground of all, with all its diverse structures, smells, textures, its creatures of all shapes and sizes, its abundant plants, some edible, others toxic. Nature offers a myriad of opportunities for risk taking, for a wealth of learning and amazement, and for freedom, separate from the adult world.

So why has our society become so disconnected from nature? Along with strangers, increasing traffic and other hazards of the modern world, nature itself is often seen as something alien, a threat to our children. Changes in the way we live, including a rise in risk-adverse parenting, as well as an increasing dependence on technology, contribute to an ever-more sedentary, indoor culture that counts increasing childhood obesity as only one of its negative impacts. While some fears may be justified, it's important to try to readdress these issues.

Forest School is one of many grassroots movements around the world that are currently aiming to connect children with nature once more. Now a global phenomenon, Forest School developed in the UK in the 1990s as both an approach to early years learning, initially inspired by the play-based, nature-centred pedagogy of Scandinavia known in Denmark as *friluftsliv* ('free open-air life'), and as an ever-growing collection of individual Forest Schools. These range from educational play schemes held in local parks and in mainstream schools to specialist programmes to help with addiction recovery and social inclusion. The Forest School Association, the independent body representing Forest

School in the UK, has provided the following definition:

'Forest School is an inspirational process, that offers all learners regular opportunities to achieve and develop confidence and self-esteem through hands-on learning experiences in a woodland or natural environment with trees.'

This approach draws on, in addition to the Scandinavian outdoor model, the learning theories and playful child-centred pedagogy of thinkers such as Rudolf Steiner and Maria Montessori, and on the nature-based education activities of Kurt Hahn and the British Scouting and Woodcraft Folk movements, among other influences. These views have relevance for Forest School today, with its ethos of therapeutic educational learning that aims to maximize social, emotional and developmental potential by allowing children to manage risk, have more independence in guiding their own learning, achieve goals, be active, play and learn through direct experience within nature. Within this context, a Forest School leader assesses each child's interests and learning styles and engages with them to facilitate their full learning ability. Outside the confines of four walls, without the distractions of electronic devices and excessive supervision, children can move, explore and discover at their own pace, connecting to the natural world – a place not created by man, that had deep spiritual meaning for our ancestors.

This book offers some fantastic games, crafts and skill-building activities from the Forest School sessions we hold in London and elsewhere, giving children who have not yet had a chance to attend Forest School a taste of what goes on there. And for children who have already discovered Forest School, this is a way of bringing those activities into their outdoor play and learning with you. Of course a book can never be a replacement for the full Forest School experience, which requires repeated sessions with an appropriately trained leader (for more about the principles of Forest School, visit the FSA website at www.forestschoolassociation.org). So we urge children who haven't already been to Forest School to try it out for themselves!

Above all, this book is about having fun in nature, especially in woodland. However, a Forest School programme aims to stimulate a child's holistic development – and for this reason we explain the learning benefits of each activity in the book. For example, using a fire steel (under adult supervision of course) is a skill that takes time, focus, patience, persistence and resilience to master. Success can truly empower a child, raising confidence to try new skills and encouraging a healthy approach to managing risk. We never tire of seeing the sheer joy flash across the face of a child who has persevered and finally triumphed in lighting a fire using just a fire steel!

Children are immensely curious and have a strong desire to play and explore the world around them, and by making choices in this way they actively drive their own learning and development. Research suggests that young children learn best from experience, by using their senses actively rather than passively, and it is via these experiences that the learning remains with us into adulthood. Providing varied outdoor experiences can help with this development. Free play gives children space and independence, and a chance to imagine and learn social skills, while adult-guided activities such as tool use build new skills, vocabulary and the ability to manage risk, creating a positive self-identity and laying foundations to be a successful lifelong learner.

HOW TO PLAY THE FOREST SCHOOL WAY!

We've written this book for parents, teachers and guardians who will take the role of the Forest School leader in being present (so put your phone away!), encouraging, inspiring and helping the activity to be achieved, at the same time letting the child lead the experience. The activities are suitable for a wide age range, from pre-school children up to about age 11, so obviously adults will need to assess the individual capabilities of each child.

We've suggested kit for each activity. In addition, bring a first-aid kit, and a supply of water, soap and paper towels for cleaning hands. Getting dirty without having to worrying about it is part of playing outdoors and activities can take place in all weathers (apart from high winds in woods), so make sure everyone is dressed appropriately in clothes that don't need to be kept clean.

Each Forest School session has a beginning and an ending, and its own flow; this framing and rhythm can provide inspiration for your own woodland activities. At Forest School, beginnings establish safety rules and the physical boundaries of the play area, and how to treat each other and the environment with respect (if you are in a protected area, check with the landowner about rare plants that should not be picked, and animals not to disturb). We also discuss issues such as where food will be kept and where to wash hands. This reflects psychologist Abraham Maslow's theory of the hierarchy of needs, in which basic needs, such as those for food, shelter, safety and community, must be met first to allow children to achieve their full potential for personal development.

One key aspect to establish before deciding on the first activity is mood and level of energy. You can ask older children to rate their feelings on a scale of 1 to 10, with 1 being no good and 10 being great. Ask small groups directly or get large groups sitting in a circle and use a talking stick (see below) to encourage them to share their thoughts and feelings. Let the words come from them, and use these and your observations as clues as you plan your session or day.

For example, if you have a group (such as a birthday party) in which some children are new to each other and the energy is high, the Wildlife Team Games (see section entitled "Wildlife Team Games") are always a fantastic way to start, channelling high spirits into working together, empathy and having plenty of fun. Any of the Nature Explorers activities (see section entitled "Nature Explorers") will help deepen the children's connection with nature, and are perfect if they are interested in finding out more about their surroundings. The crafts in Forest Arts (see section entitled "Forest Arts") are great when the energy level is focused, perhaps following a round of games – or after lunch on a hot day! There is also a whole chapter on Survival Skills (see section entitled "Survival Skills") – training in any of these can be transformational in raising self-esteem. The more familiar you become with the activities, the easier it will be to switch between them as needed to respond to the natural flow of the day and the feelings of those involved.

> ## TRY THIS!
> **With a large group, diffuse possible arguments by pulling names out of a bag to choose roles in a game.**

As we do at Forest School, make sure there are enough adults present to allow children to play and undertake achievable, challenging activities in a safe, nurturing space. This also provides an opportunity to observe each child's interests and learning styles, useful for when you are planning future play sessions. Some activities require more than one child to take part; if that's the case, the ideal number of players is suggested.

At the start of each activity, read through the instructions, demonstrate any tricky techniques, and then let the child as far as possible attempt each step, offering positive encouragement, and only assist if required. Knowing that kids love to work things out for themselves, we've designed the step-by-step instructions and diagrams to be as simple and easily grasped as possible. As the activity progresses, let the child lead and be mindful not to impose your own views. If someone wants to tie an old sweet wrapper onto a wand, for example, let them do that rather than seeing it as rubbish! Only if something is harmful or dangerous is intervention required, but in an explanatory, empowering way.

At Forest School, at the end of a session we ask the children to say how they now feel. To consolidate learning, facilitate deeper thinking and encourage them to play an active part in their own learning, children are also given the opportunity to reflect on their experiences. What did they learn? What did they like and what did they find challenging? We have made some suggestions for ending discussions to close each activity. As well as helping the children's learning, these discussions are a fantastic way of gaining insight into learning styles and into what worked and what could possibly be changed, providing a guide for future sessions. Rounding up in this way also allows everyone to let go of the play and move into a different space, within themselves as well as physically.

TRY THIS!

To give everyone a chance to make their voice heard, sit in a circle and use a 'talking stick'. This can be any chosen stick but it empowers the holder to speak and have respect from others, who

> **must be quiet and listen until they themselves have a turn. Magic!**

We know more now about nature than ever before: how ecosystems work, how species can become extinct. This knowledge is incredibly important for the future wellbeing of the planet and its people, but if generations to come are to have the desire to put this knowledge into practice then they must feel a connection to nature, which can only be achieved through meaningful experience in the natural world. And what could be more memorable than learning joyfully through outdoor play? The fully immersed experience of being in the elements, with trusted adults and friends, is just one part of what Forest School aims to achieve.

xiii

Nature Explorers

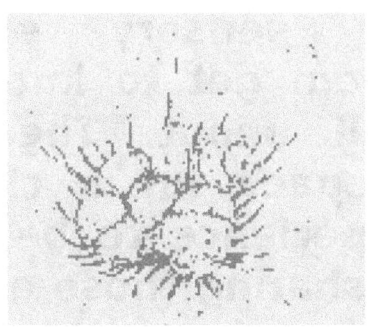

All the activities in this chapter offer children an opportunity to encounter the natural world through new imaginative experiences, to become fully immersed in an outdoor environment.

These fun, active games get the kids using all their abilities and senses. They inspire them to investigate their surroundings and also to explore their thoughts and feelings, whether these are their own or those of different species. Sometimes this means imagining the behaviour of different animals or comparing like with like; sometimes it involves taking away one sense to open up new ways of perceiving. Blindfolded and face to face with a tree, a child will be struck by the feel of the damp moss, by the smell of the wood ... all these sensory experiences helping them get to know what a tree is all about. The activities create a space for a child's own unique experience to be valid and right, and sharing those experiences with others develops trust and empathy.

From play comes real knowledge about the environment and a direct connection with nature, a sense of belonging, of wonder and of respect for life. Cherished memories form, along with an enthusiasm to return and experience more, and through this a lasting sense of stewardship for our amazing, unique natural world is born.

JOURNEY STICK

Tradition says the Aboriginal people of Australia once created journey sticks to record their travels and help them retell their stories to others. On each journey stick they would tie different objects that represented the places they visited, as well as the feelings, thoughts and experiences they had along the way.

What's magical about a journey stick is that each one is unique. There is no right or wrong way of making it. All our journeys are different, and so are the ways we remember and represent them.

A leaf may be a reminder of a sunbeam breaking through the woodland canopy, warming the skin. A feather may call to mind a burst of bird song; a pebble, a feeling. An acorn may summon up the image of an old oak tree passed on the journey. Even the different colours of the rubber bands or lengths of wool used in this activity to tie on items can represent places, thoughts and feelings.

This walk activity allows children to run around and feel free, picking up whatever captures their interest. It's creative and imaginative. It focuses the attention on being truly present, on looking, hearing and feeling what's around, and what this means to them. It develops curiosity in the natural world, as well as the communication skills and empathy needed to retell a journey and listen to the stories of others. Attaching objects to the stick also helps to develop fine motor skills.

I'm always surprised to see what children choose to tie on their journey sticks. My own son went for an old red tennis ball that a dog had chewed in half! My knee-jerk reaction was, 'Don't touch, that's dirty!' but I reminded myself that it posed no threat and that his journey stick belonged to him. The discarded ball was then transformed into an interesting, colourful object with a fuzzy texture, and stood out brightly on the stick. Discarded sweet wrappers, lost balls, bird feathers ... all have their creative value!

LOCATION	Woodland is ideal, as this offers lots of sticks, as well as great biodiversity and varied terrain, but any natural environment is suitable.
AGE GROUP	4 years +
LEARNING ABOUT ...	Imagination ❀ creativity ❀ focus ❀ curiosity ❀ using fine motor skills ❀ empathy ❀ connecting with nature ❀ communication
KIT	→ Sticks (if fallen ones are not available on the ground) → Lengths of string/wool in different colours → Rubber bands in different colours

Get ready

Have a route in mind for your walk, with a beginning and an end point. Tell everyone they're about to go on a journey that they might want to tell their friends and family about afterwards. Their journey stick will help them remember it. Then gather your journey sticks. Everyone should find and choose their own stick – one that is easy to handle and stands out for them.

Younger children may have trouble tying string, so it can be helpful to wind rubber bands round the stick to tuck things into. If you have a selection of colours, they can pick their favourites. Let older children choose handfuls of differently coloured string, as well as the bands. These can be used to attach things to the sticks and the colours may also help with remembering different experiences.

Get set

Tell the children they're going to be gathering natural objects and things that they like on their journey, to become part of their sticks. As they are walking they can think about the sounds they hear, any feelings and thoughts, the landscapes, trees and animals that catch their attention, the smells, the route they are following. The things they collect will help them remember these experiences.

Remind everyone what is OK to pick up and what is not, such as rare or poisonous plants, or dangerous items such as broken glass.

Go!

Head off on your journey! Put the first thing found at the top of the stick to represent the beginning and the last thing found near the middle or bottom of the stick. This will help with retelling the story of the journey.

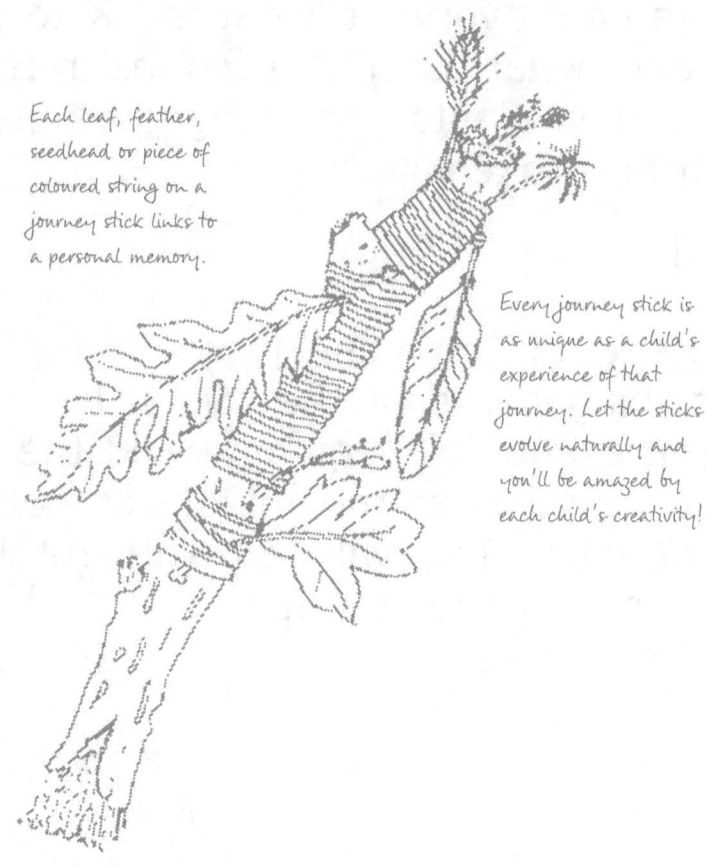

Each leaf, feather, seedhead or piece of coloured string on a journey stick links to a personal memory.

Every journey stick is as unique as a child's experience of that journey. Let the sticks evolve naturally and you'll be amazed by each child's creativity!

Endings

First take time to admire each journey stick, talking about how colourful, interesting, beautiful and unique the stick has become. Encourage each child to tell the others about their journey, using the various objects as prompts to remind them of the story. If anyone struggles, ask why they chose those things, which one is their favourite and why, and where it was found. Talk about the chosen items. Where do they come from? What do the plants or animals use them for? And what can we do to ensure these plants and animals are still around in the future?

WOODLAND MAPPING

Imagine actually living in a forest ... this is your home, the place that provides you with food and shelter. You may have to find a stream for water, a bush with edible berries or a fallen tree for firewood and sticks to build a shelter. But in a wood it can be difficult to see what's around you, with leafy trees, dense bushes and uneven ground blocking the view. This fantastic game is all about really getting to know a natural place. Working as a team like ants, the children will be a search party, combing an area for what it provides and using their finds to create a map of the surroundings.

This activity provides an opportunity to teach survival skills (see section entitled "Survival Skills"), showing that human survival has always been linked to the land and an understanding of it, and to co-operating in a community with other people. It creates a strong bond with the environment and develops curiosity and focus, as the children collect objects and look at their potential uses. It's also a good opportunity to introduce children to the naming of plants, enhancing memory and language skills as they discuss where they found them and their possible benefits. Through pacing out the area to be mapped and visually representing it, children can also develop an understanding of distance, scale and location. And, best of all, imagination unfolds whether the children see themselves as birds scanning for food as they soar above the trees, or as scouting ants searching the ground or as a nomadic tribe exploring a new territory for what they need.

Get ready

Set up a base camp for the time you are in the woods – this is your forest home. Everyone will be exploring the area around this home, looking for natural items that catch their attention (avoiding rare or poisonous plants) and using these things to map out on the ground exactly what can be found in the surroundings.

LOCATION	Woodland
AGE GROUP	6 years +
NUMBER OF PLAYERS	Ideally 4 +, to cover all the directions, but this is not essential
LEARNING ABOUT ...	Connecting with nature ✿ curiosity ✿ focus ✿ teamwork ✿ identification skills ✿ memory ✿ language ✿ imagination ✿ distance, location and scale ✿ sustainability
KIT	→ Sticks (if fallen ones are not available on the ground) → Pencils/pens and small sticky notes (for younger children, optional)

Get set

All members of the team need to find a stick that's as long as their arm and another that's roughly half this size. Arrange the long sticks on the ground like the spokes of a wheel, and then put the shorter sticks around the outside to create the edge of the wheel.

Once the wheel is made, stand in front of your small stick. Behind you on the ground should be a triangle formed by two long sticks and one short one. This triangle is where you will place five things that you find as you walk forward for around 50m (165ft) (less if space is limited or with younger children).

Go!

Walk forward in a straight line for about 10m (33ft) – try measuring this in paces – and stop. Pick up something you can see, perhaps a leaf, a stick, a rock, a nutshell or a pine cone. Now walk straight onward for another 10m (33ft) and repeat. Continue until you have walked 50m (165ft) and collected five things. Remember their order. If you spot water, remember which item was closest to it.

Once you have collected your five objects, walk back to the stick wheel. Place the first thing you found closest to the centre of the wheel, then the second a bit further out and so on until you put the fifth object near the outer short stick. If you saw water, draw a wiggly snake line in the soil next to whatever you collected near it. You now have a fantastic map showing

TRY THIS!

Use small sticky notes to number the objects if younger children find it difficult to remember the order of their finds. the position of the plants, rocks, water and other natural things in a 50m (165ft) circle around the camp!

Endings

Now that you have completed the map, ask the children how they think it can be used. Discuss the objects they found – what uses do they have in nature? How they might benefit humans and other animals? Does anyone have a favourite object? Why? You could also talk about what we humans need to survive in a forest. What materials do we require to build a shelter, for example? (For ideas about shelters, see section entitled "BUILDING SHELTERS".) What plants are safe for us to eat? (For more on wild food, see section entitled "WILD FOOD".) Finally, you could talk together about how a forest can be managed in a sustainable way, for example by not overlogging and by controlling invasive nonnative species, such as rhododendron in native British woodlands.

ACORN HIDE-AND-SEEK

Have you ever wondered why a squirrel's cheeks are full when it's digging up the ground? It's probably hiding acorns! Like some other woodland animals, including chipmunks and jays, squirrels collect food in autumn to eat in the winter months when supplies are scarce. Wary of onlookers who may steal their stash, they roam far and wide to bury their hoards in lots of different places. As they do, they have even been known to fool potential thieves by turning their backs on these spies and making dummy caches, containing no acorns at all. When the squirrels return months later to find their food hoards, they rely on their memory and keen senses, smelling these buried treasures underground!

Who can survive as a squirrel? Let's find out!

This physically active game is also about using memory, focus and self-control to achieve a specific goal – finding the hidden acorns. It's a fun activity that raises self-esteem, teaching players that persistence brings success, and a great opportunity to explore and connect with nature. And as the children take on the role of a squirrel, the world of animal make-believe comes to life!

Get ready

Imagine yourselves as squirrels in autumn, gathering acorns and hiding them so you can dig them up and eat them in the winter months when there's not much food around. Think about choosing a good hiding place that other squirrels and anything else interested in your hoard (such as birds) won't find.

LOCATION	Any woodland or park where there are squirrels and acorns in autumn is ideal. If you can't find any acorns, you could use hazelnuts or beech mast instead.
AGE GROUP	3 years +
LEARNING ABOUT ...	Focus ⊛ self-control ⊛ memory ⊛ self-esteem ⊛ being active ⊛ imagination ⊛ forest ecology
KIT	A small bag or container for each child (for collecting acorns)

With this in mind each squirrel finds an oak tree and collects five to ten acorns from the forest floor beneath it, putting them in the bag or container. For the younger ones five acorns will do.

Get set

Now you have your acorns, look around and find a good place to hide them. Make sure that no one else sees where you stash them. A good hiding spot might be behind or under a rock, buried next to a puddle, in a tree hole or near a fallen log. Remember these and other details of the surroundings – whatever will help you find your hiding place again.

Once this is done, everyone goes for a walk in the surrounding area. (To limit potential frustration, keep the walk short for younger children.) Then it's time to head back to where those tasty acorns were hidden.

Go!

Now find your acorns! Are they still there? Can the squirrels discover them all?

> ### TRY THIS!
> **To bury acorns, use a stick to dig a small, shallow hole, put them in and cover them with earth or fallen leaves.**

Offer hints and praise, particularly if anyone is struggling, but let the squirrels find their stash themselves.

Endings

Ask the children to describe how it felt to be a squirrel. What skills do they think a squirrel needs to survive? Why did they choose their particular hiding places? Was it easy to find their acorns again? What helped them to find them? What did they find difficult and why?

Explain that squirrels can recognize each other, as well as food, by smell. Tell them about other foods that squirrels like to eat, such as hazelnuts, beech mast, tree bark, fungi, buds, leaves and flowers. Older children may be intrigued to learn that squirrels sometimes raid birds' nests for their eggs and young. (See below for more information about squirrels and oak trees.)

Acorns have even been consumed by humans! During World War II, when food was in short supply, people drank a coffee substitute made from processed acorns, which were just as easy to gather then as they are now. (Just in case anyone is thinking of trying to eat an acorn, it might be an idea to point out that the nuts taste very bitter, so it's best not to eat them raw!)

SCAVENGER HUNT

Children have a natural urge to explore. A scavenger hunt is a fun, structured way of focusing this curiosity on all the shapes, sounds, plants, animals and other elements of their surroundings, opening the door to identification and deepening their bond with the landscape around them. This activity creates a sense of knowing, of familiarity, which in turn leads to a feeling of belonging, of being at home in the natural world.

By making connections between what is sought and what is found, children learn how one thing relates to another and hone the use of their senses. This can lay the building blocks for recognizing themes in other areas, such as reading and mathematics, helping children to sort, process and use information in a variety of settings. They also learn to make connections between their inner experiences and the external world. And all this through play!

Get ready

Coming up with ideas for a scavenger hunt is easy: just think of outdoor objects that are common in your chosen area. (Obviously, avoid anything rare or poisonous!) You can also include experiences – for example, hearing a specific sound or feeling the wind on your face. Before you play, design a clue card with 9–16 things to find (adjust the number according to the age of the children and time available). Your clues could be pictures or just words or both pictures and words – see the example below, which you can photocopy and use if it works for your area. You could cut pictures from a magazine or download them from the Internet and print them out, then mount the pieces of paper onto sturdy cards. Alternatively, draw and write your clues straight onto the cards.

To protect the clue cards, especially if you suspect it might be rainy, slot them into plastic sleeves. To allow the hunters to keep their hands free, string thread (enough to loop around the head and shoulders and allow the clues to be easily viewed) through holes in the card or through the protective sleeve.

LOCATION	Any woodland or other natural area (such as a beach) that offers a good selection of animals, birds, plants and trees is ideal. However, with some planning you can make this game work in any environment.
AGE GROUP	3 years +
LEARNING ABOUT ...	Using the senses ❀ being active ❀ focus ❀ recognizing themes ❀ connecting with nature ❀ ecology
KIT	→ A scavenger clue card for each child/team → Clear plastic sleeves to protect clue cards (optional – depends on weather/terrain) → String for wearing the cards around the neck (optional) → Pencils

Get set

Check in with all the hunters to make sure they understand the clues.

You can make the hunt more challenging for older kids by adding a time limit, but keep any targets achievable so the children stay interested and don't get frustrated. Bigger groups can, if they wish, be divided into teams but bear in mind that some kids may prefer to hunt alone.

Go!

Off the hunters go! Get them to put crosses through the clues as they find them. Don't be afraid to join in as a helper to liven things up and provide encouragement and hints. For example, you could ask, 'Was that a squirrel up there?' or 'Where do you think you might find an acorn?'. But always let the kids take the initiative and do the hunting themselves!

Endings

When you have finished, talk through the hunt with the children. What was the hardest thing to find? What was each child's favourite? Was there anything they couldn't track down and why? How did hunting and finding the items make them feel? You can provide some interesting facts about the clues to add to the enthusiasm and enhance the children's connection with nature. Here are a few to get you started:

- English oaks live on average for 500 years, but there's an oak in Bulgaria that's 1,700 years old.
- Grey squirrels can jump 3m (10ft) from one tree to the next. (For more information on squirrels and acorns, see above.)

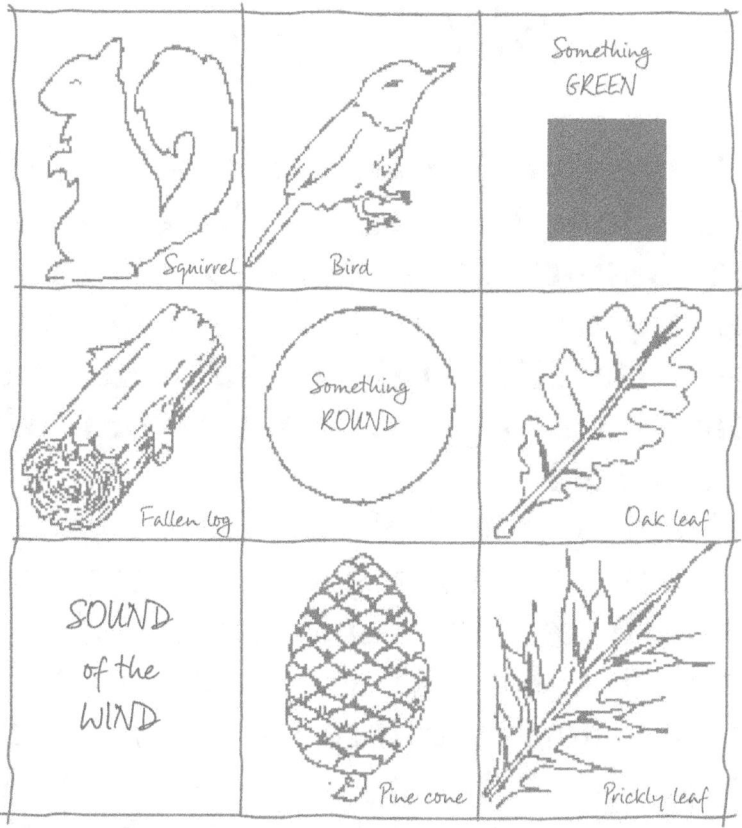

- Prickly leaves can protect plants from some grazing animals.
- A decaying log is a home for many insects, mosses, lichens and fungi, which in turn can provide food for other species such as birds, who love to eat insects.

Allow the children to fully express their thoughts and continue the discussion until it runs its natural course.

MY TREE

Have you ever come quietly, eyes closed, face to face with a tree, using your senses of touch, hearing and smell to explore its every detail? And would you know your tree again, just from this encounter?

This game offers an amazing personal experience that not only demonstrates the uniqueness of each tree that makes up a woodland but also allows children to forge their own deep connection with one of these forest friends. As one child leads the other blindfolded through the wood to a chosen tree, a bond of trust and empathy is created, and steady focus is required of both as one acts for the eyes of the other. The journey is full of excitement and anticipation, and culminates in an experience of the different textures and smells of a tree. Then comes the ultimate challenge: can the children find their tree again, drawing on what they sensed, felt, smelled and heard during the journey and their meeting with the tree? For us, the highlights are watching the guide giggle and jump around as their partner tries to find their tree, the children's delight in their achievement when it's located and their wonder at seeing the forest in a new light. Unforgettable!

Get ready

Choose an area that is as free as possible from low-lying branches, prickly bushes, trip hazards and so on. Before you start, decide how far the children will walk through woodland. A distance of about 20m (65ft) is about right for younger players, but older children can try going further.

LOCATION	Trees are the key ingredient! Broadleaf woodland with a variety of tree species is best, but other areas with a good number and variety of trees, such as parks and fields, are also suitable.
AGE GROUP	4 years +
NUMBER OF PLAYERS	2 + (ideally an even number to make up pairs)
LEARNING ABOUT ...	Being active ⊛ using the senses ⊛ deduction ⊛ focus ⊛ self-reliance ⊛ connecting with nature ⊛ significant personal experience ⊛ empathy ⊛ teamwork ⊛ forest habitat
KIT	A cotton scarf or other blindfold per team

Get set

Everyone pairs up and decides who will be blindfolded first and who will act as the guide. The guide is going to choose a tree and lead their blindfolded partner to it. Everyone can play at the same time or you can all watch as each pair has a turn. Remind the guides to be kind to their blindfolded partners – they will be next!

Go!

Guides now lead their partners through the forest at a slow, steady pace, helping them to avoid all obstacles along the way. Each guide chooses a tree, one that stands out to them from all the rest, and places their blindfolded partner's hands on the trunk to start exploring it.

To help their partner really get to know the tree, a guide can ask questions such as: 'Does the bark feel smooth, rough or bumpy?', 'Does the tree feel like it's living?', 'Does it smell of anything?', 'Can you feel or smell any plants growing on it?', 'Does it seem big or small?', 'Can you find any leaves or branches?', 'Do the roots stick out above ground?'

After the tree exploration is finished, guides take their partners back to the start point, following a roundabout route to make finding the tree again a little more difficult. (To make it easier for younger children, take them back along the same route.) Once back, the children take off their blindfolds ... now let them try to find that special tree!

When the tree is found, each pair swaps roles. It's now the guide's turn to be blindfolded!

> **TRY THIS!**
>
> **If anyone finds it hard to locate their tree, help by saying 'hotter' when they get closer and 'colder' when they are moving further away!**

Endings

Encourage the children to discuss their experience and think about what helped them find their tree. How did they link their sense of touch to their sense of sight? You could ask questions such as: 'Did anything you walked across help guide you back to your tree?' 'What was the most difficult part?' 'Why?' 'What feature of your tree aided you most in identifying it?' 'When you finally saw your tree, what did you notice first?' 'Did you see anything that you'd expected to be different?' Explain that our sense of smell is closely linked to memory – so did this help in locating their tree?

Identifying all the trees the guides chose will help create a sense of knowing and familiarity with these amazing forms of life. When you leave the woodland, see if you can spot similar species along the way. Talk about all the things trees give us – dry, dead branches are great for fire making; some trees produce edible nuts and fruits; trees provide shade on a hot day; wood pulp is used to make paper and timber for building. Most importantly, trees create oxygen and their leaves trap pollution, keeping our air clean; their roots also prevent soil erosion and they can reduce noise pollution. Trees also provide a home for numerous other species – beetles, mosses, birds and dormice, to name but a few. They are not only beautiful but crucial for our survival!

PHOTOGRAPHIC MEMORY

This game has its lively aspect, encouraging children to dash about trying to locate the objects they've 'photographed'. But it also harnesses their energy, quietens distracting thoughts and creates space to become mindful of and interested in the natural world around them. And of course it offers them an opportunity to test out and improve their memory, too!

Each player takes on the role of a camera, fixing in their mind a picture of some natural objects that they are shown. By looking closely at the items, identifying what they are and then tracking down similar specimens in their environment, the children gain direct experience of these objects and feel a real sense of connection with them, which in turn can lead to truly valuing and caring for nature. The ability to observe similarities and differences and associate one thing with another is a skill that can be helpful in other areas, such as when learning the alphabet in the early years and later on in writing and mathematics.

And as with other challenges, completing this one helps children to develop self-reliance and confidence. We have found this game creates great camaraderie, the players laughing and yelling to each other whenever they find what they're looking for!

Get ready

Without the children seeing what you are collecting, gather five to ten common natural objects from the area, such as a rock, a pine cone, a stick, a nutshell, a blade of grass and so on (nothing rare or poisonous). For younger kids, choose five objects as this amount will be easier to remember and find, helping to prevent frustration.

Arrange the objects on one of the cloths and cover them with the other cloth. Now ask the players to imagine they are a camera. When you remove the cloth they are going to keep their eyes focused like a lens on the objects under the cloth for 30 seconds. They will then shut their eyes tight (as if pressing the shutter button!) and take a mental picture of all the things they have seen.

LOCATION	Any natural space offering a diverse range of plants, trees, birds and animals
AGE GROUP	5 years +
NUMBER OF PLAYERS	2 + (including 1 adult)
LEARNING ABOUT ...	Memory ✺ making connections/categorizing ✺ focus ✺ being active ✺ connecting with the natural world ✺ teamwork
KIT	→ 2 cloths, big enough to display/cover 10 objects → 1 small bag per player/team (or objects can just be carried)

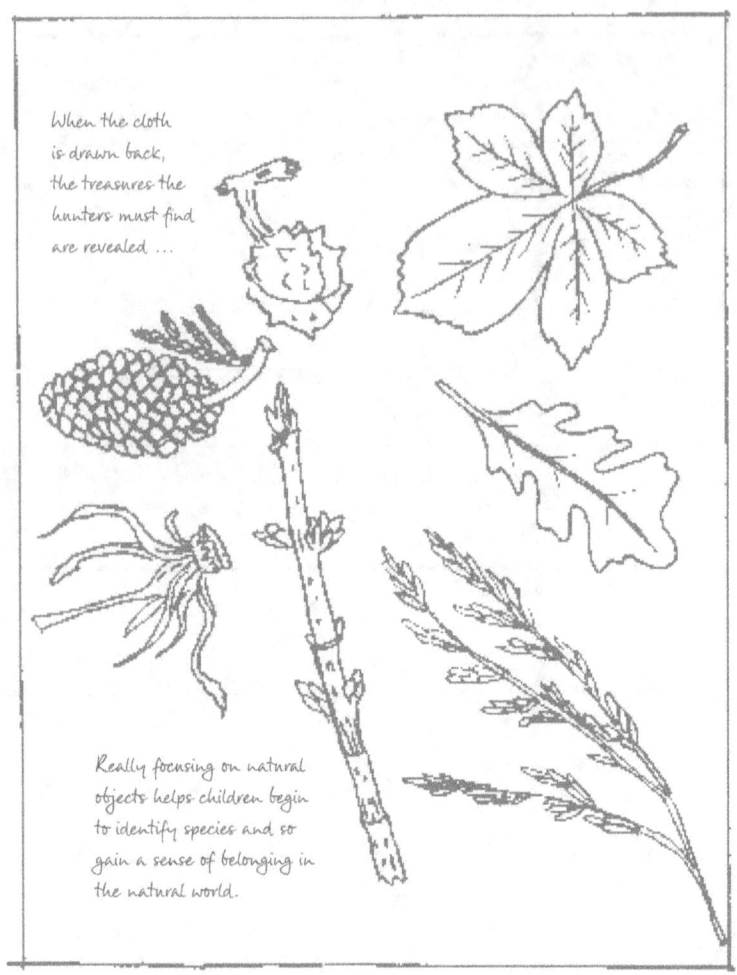

When the cloth is drawn back, the treasures the hunters must find are revealed …

Really focusing on natural objects helps children begin to identify species and so gain a sense of belonging in the natural world.

Get set

Whisk away the cloth so the children can get a good look at the objects. After 30 seconds cover up the objects again while the children shut their eyes to take a 'photograph'. Ask them to hold this picture in their mind.

Go!

Looking at their mental picture, the children head off to find an example of each of the objects they 'photographed', placing them in the bag if they have one. After 10–20 minutes of searching, call the players back with the things they've found so they can lay them out in front of the covered objects. Now, take out one object at a time from under the cloth, hold it up and ask if anyone found something similar.

Endings

Talk about each item – what it is and where it came from. Discuss its uniqueness, its possible uses and benefits for humans and for other species and, if relevant, its sustainable management. For example, if you have included any grasses, you can talk about how a grassland habitat could be maintained to help the species who live there survive, such as by regular cutting to prevent it turning into woodland.

If anyone wants to find something they missed, encourage them to look again. Repeating the whole game helps players to develop their memory and ability to focus.

Forest Arts

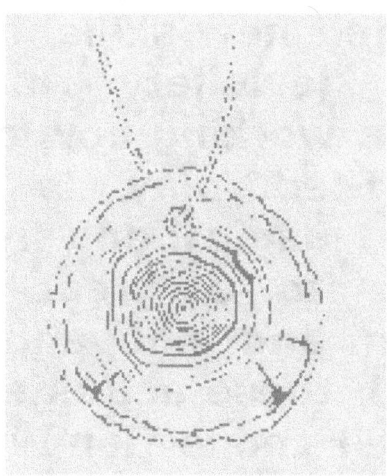

Today, ready-made plastic toys and the virtual worlds of computer games, with predetermined uses and outcomes, are the norm for children's play. The art and craft activities in this chapter place no such restrictions on a child's thinking or creativity. Each item's nature and look are determined by its maker, and these unique works of art in turn stimulate a world of make-believe, role play and storytelling. The possibilities are as limitless as each child's creativity.

Working with the natural materials found on the forest floor, these activities encourage focus, determination, patience and responsibility. The children take pride in their new skills, from using tools in jewellery making to designing a working bow and arrow. This child-led play is inclusive, achievable, magical and freeing, and gives rise to a great sense of self-esteem and independence.

Through these activities children deepen their connection with nature, directly as well as scientifically, historically and through folklore. Nature taps into an ancient place within us all, and absorption in creative activities in a natural place gives children a unique space in which to explore, express and work through their ideas and feelings, in a way that would not be possible in other settings.

MAGIC WANDS

What could be more magical than a wand? Deeply rooted in ancient symbolism, wands are an essential accessory for many of the fantastical beings of myth and folktale, with unrivalled status as an instrument of powerful magic. Stories abound of wands being used to transform people into animals and make objects move or vanish, among a myriad of other tricks. Whether you are a fairy-in-waiting, a witch with a mission or a wizard with a grudge, a world of spells, conjuring and transformation awaits!

Some wands are made from crystal and others from metal, but at Forest School the wands are wood – a material that itself is deeply imbued with symbolism. The Ogham alphabet (see examples below) of the ancient Celts associated letters with native trees, with each tree linked to various energies and qualities. The silver birch, for example, symbolized transformation and new beginnings. One of the first trees to colonize a grassland, its sparse foliage permits others plants to grow beneath it. Its leaves and twigs fall to the ground and nourish the soil, so that seeds from other plants and longer-living trees, such as oak, begin to grow and an empty grassland becomes a majestic forest. The stately and long-lived oak, on the other hand, is a symbol of strength, endurance and courage. The yew has a lifespan that exceeds even that of the oak, and represents death and rebirth. This tree has a remarkable strategy for regeneration, rotting away from within its trunk at around 800 years old but living on as its branches grow downward to form new roots. Elder was believed, in Scandinavia, to protect against witchcraft, while elsewhere it was a means to see faery folk! Some knowledge of the Ogham alphabet and other tree folklore can add an exciting extra level of meaning to wand creation, imbuing a wand made of birch, for example, with the power of transformation.

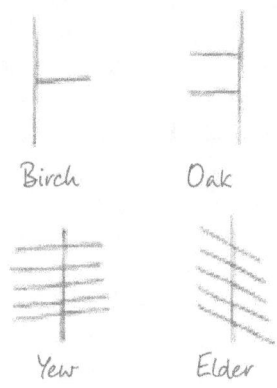

Talking about the choice of stick for the wand builds identification skills, deepening a child's sense of connection with the natural world. Designing and decorating a wand is a wonderfully creative activity that develops communication and fine motor skills, builds confidence and, above all, fires the imagination.

LOCATION	Any natural space with a variety of tree species – woodland is ideal, but parks and gardens with fallen sticks to play with will work, too.
AGE GROUP	4 years +
LEARNING ABOUT…	Tree identification ❂ fine motor skills ❂ being creative ❂ using the imagination ❂ myth and folklore ❂ connecting with nature ❂ self-confidence ❂ communication
KIT	→ Sticks (if fallen ones are not available on the ground) → Coloured wool, ideally in four or five different colours → Scissors (optional)

Get ready

Tell everyone how ancient peoples all over the world believed that trees have special powers. A wand made from wood captures the tree's powers and transfers the magic to the wand-bearer. How will they use their wands and who will they be when they use them?

Get set

Everyone heads off to find a stick that's perfect for their wand. It could have fallen from a tree that has special powers in folklore or perhaps it's just a stick they like, leaving them free to dream up its powers for themselves. (If there is a chance anyone will create a wand from the magical yew, remind them that yew is poisonous for humans to eat.) Nobbles and gnarly knots on the stick all add to the character of the finished wand. Also search for natural decorations to adorn the wands. The children can pick up anything they like from the forest floor, such as feathers, leaves and seeds, only avoiding poisonous or rare plants.

Go!

When they are happy with the materials for their wands, the wand-makers can choose some coloured wool to attach decorative objects. Tie these on with a double overhand knot (see section entitled "Overhand knot"). Winding on wool is another way to make the wand unique. Again, tie one end to the stick with a double overhand knot (younger children may need help with this). The wool can then be wound around the stick until the loose end is of the desired length. Secure at the other end with another double overhand knot. How all this is done is up to the wand maker.

Wool can be wound around the stick in circles or in a crisscross pattern. Even the different colours might have special powers of their own ...

Now it's time to cast some spells. Let the magic begin!

Endings

Encourage the children in turn to describe their wand. What are its magical powers? What features of the wand provide these powers? How does holding the wand make them feel?

Looking at the different sticks used to make the wands, you could discuss how every tree has its own distinctive features. A birch tree, for example, has white bark, which makes it easy to tell apart from other trees in a forest. Can you spot the trees the sticks came from?

Ask the children to tell you about the characters they've read about or seen in movies or on television who use wands – what magical powers do they have? Are these used for good or for mischief?

MUD FACES

There is such joy in squeezing and squelching mud through the fingers! Shaping a face from mud is blissful messy play. With a little imagination, this activity populates the trees with strange inhabitants and brings the forest alive in a whole new way.

Mixing together the elements of earth and water to create a mud face taps into every child's instinct to investigate natural things, and explore what these do and how they react. This activity combines art, science and sensory development, encourages communication and confidence through creativity, and also gives children permission to get really mucky! Studies show that being able to get dirty is an important part of a child's cognitive development. There are health benefits, too: safe exposure to natural organisms in soil helps to develop children's immune systems, making them more able to fight disease.

This may be the first time a child has been given the freedom to get really muddy. Some may relish this, while others may for a time feel it's a challenge. Repeatedly giving permission and encouragement can ease this worry to joy. Ask any adults involved in the activity to be enthusiastic, to let go any of their concerns over muddy play – the children will wash their hands afterwards.

This activity allows the children to explore and connect with their environment, whether they are looking for grass or ferns for hair, stones for teeth or nuts for eyes. Mixing, concocting and creating takes everyone back to the realm of invention and magic: the entire activity is full of possibilities for imaginative expression. A wonderfully creative, liberating activity!

LOCATION	Any natural area with soil and trees. For atmosphere, woodland is ideal.
AGE GROUP	2 years +
LEARNING ABOUT …	Imagination ✿ using the senses ✿ fine motor skills ✿ science ✿ art ✿ being creative ✿ communicating ✿ empathy ✿ connecting with nature ✿ confidence
KIT	→ Waterproofs and/or clothing for messy play → Suitable footwear → A trowel or small spade per player → A small bucket or other watertight container per player → Water (for mixing mud) → Soap and clean water (for washing hands afterwards) or lots of wet wipes until you can get to a tap!

Get ready

Encourage the children to talk about their ideas. Will it be a mud face for a tree, an animal or an insect? Will it be the face of someone they know, or the face of a character in a story or a magical being they've invented? Will it have big or small eyes? Perhaps there will be more than two eyes! What about ears? And hair – will it be fuzzy or straight or will there be none at all? Maybe the face will turn into a creature with arms, hands, legs and toes!

Get set

When everyone has had a turn talking about what their mud creation will be, head off to gather the materials. Perhaps they'll pick up acorns or horse chestnuts for eyes, leaves for ears, or sticks for mouths. Tiny feathers may be perfect for hair. Or perhaps they'll choose something completely unexpected. The makers decide! (Just avoid any rare or poisonous plants!)

Once they have gathered all they need, the children can use a trowel or small spade to dig a hole past the topsoil, down to the mulch-free soil (roughly 5–20cm/2–8in deep). Each child digs out enough soil to quarter-fill their bucket, then slowly adds water until they have sticky mud, the consistency of workable clay. Stickiness can be tested on a tree trunk – if the mud sticks, it's just right. (More soil and water can always be added if needed.)

Go!

All the makers find a tree where their creation will live, then takes a good handful of mud from their bucket and shape it into a ball. Smaller children, with their little hands, may need help getting a ball that's big enough for shaping. Now the ball of mud gets splatted firmly onto the tree trunk. Press down the edges of the mud, so that it holds firmly onto the tree.

Once the ball is stuck, the creative magic begins! Let each child work on their face or creature as they wish. Watch as aliens, fairies, robots, animals and other weird and wonderful creatures emerge, each with their own lively expression and strange features.

Endings

If the children feel like talking about their creations, encourage them to do so, each taking a turn while others listen, following the story wherever it leads. Ask the children to describe and name the natural items. Where did they find them? Why were they chosen?

Remember to say goodbye to all the faces before you leave. If the weather is dry, mud faces can last for several days, so consider coming back to visit them!

NATURE'S HEADDRESSES

From ancient Egypt to the jungles and plains of Africa and the Americas, kings, queens, chiefs and shamans have worn ceremonial headdresses since time immemorial. Spectacular headdresses also have their place among celebrations such as carnivals but even a simple adornment, such as a garland of flowers or a crown of autumn leaves, has the power to transform its wearer into a noble monarch, a woodland fairy or some other magical character.

Nature provides all the materials you need for wonderful headdresses. Acorns and pretty small stones can make beautiful jewels; leaves, flowers and feathers add colour; lightweight twigs add height and stature. Running around to find these embellishments provides an outlet not only for energetic play, but also for imagination, creativity and artistic flair. Assessing all these different natural objects sharpens powers of observation and encourages curiosity. The process of piecing together the headdress hones fine motor skills, while the end result of a valued and unique piece of art inspires role play and self-esteem. Talking through the creative decisions for each headdress encourages communication, and can even lead to some quite sophisticated discussion about art and symbolism. All in all, making natural headdresses is a continuously inventive and fun process that unfolds into many magical performances.

Get ready

Each participant chooses a length of card. Measure each strip to make sure it fits round the child's head and trim off any excess (leave a bit of an overlap). Older children can do this measuring and trimming themselves. Cut double-sided sticky tape to length and stick it along the centre of each strip of card. Younger children may need help getting the length of tape in the right position but let them try.

Leave the protective strip on the uppermost side of the sticky tape until the children are ready to start sticking on all the things they find.

LOCATION	Woodland supplies a diverse range of decorative and structural materials, although any natural space where natural objects can be found will do.
AGE GROUP	3 years +
LEARNING ABOUT ...	Being creative ❂ imagination ❂ focus and curiosity ❂ fine motor skills ❂ being active ❂ communication ❂ self-esteem ❂ using the senses
KIT	→ Long strips of sturdy plain and coloured card – about 7.5–10cm (3–4in) wide and long enough to go round each child's head → Scissors → Double-sided sticky tape → Stapler/single-sided tape

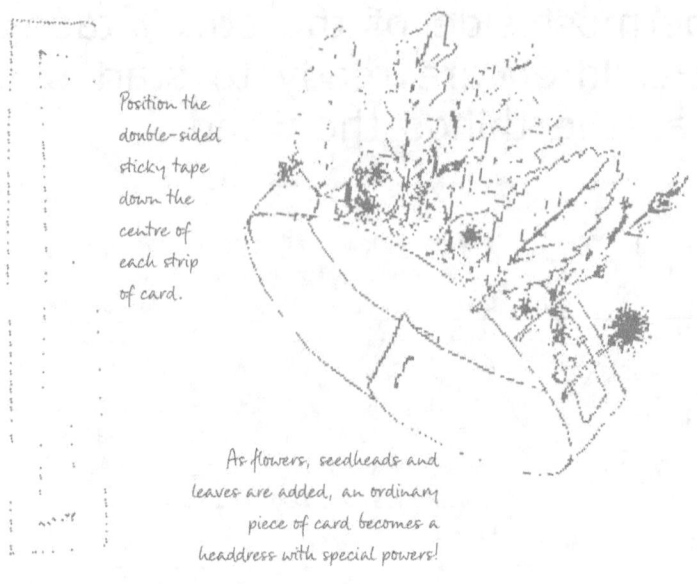

Position the double-sided sticky tape down the centre of each strip of card.

As flowers, seedheads and leaves are added, an ordinary piece of card becomes a headdress with special powers!

Get set

Talk together about the sorts of decorative things the children might be able to find and attach with sticky tape to their headdresses. Remind everyone to try to use things that are already on the forest floor and to avoid picking any rare or poisonous plants. Now remove the protective strip from the sticky tape.

Go!

The headdress-makers head off to find their decorations, sticking on flowers, seedheads, leaves and other chosen items as they find them, and watching the plain strip of card change as the headdress takes shape. As each headdress is completed, the ends can be fastened together using a stapler or single-sided sticky tape. Now each maker can wear a unique headdress with pride and feel its transformative energy!

Endings

Talk about and admire each headdress in turn. Where did the natural items used as decorations come from and what was their role in the natural world? Do they symbolize anything now they are part of the headdress? Which decoration is each child's favourite? How do the children feel when they wear their headdresses? Who or what have they become?

These questions can lead to a discussion about how we use headwear to express many different things. For example, the feathers on the headdress of a Native American chief may have been awarded for good deeds or for acts of courage. On an imperial crown, a ruby may be used to symbolize nobility.

Can anyone think of animals that make beautiful works of art? You could talk about the male bowerbirds from Australia and New Guinea, who attract mates by building elaborate structures called bowers. The birds artfully decorate these with a range of different objects that they find in their forest habitat, from flowers and moss to mounds of shiny beetle wing-cases and even discarded fizzy drink cans – showing that even something we think of as trash can become art.

ICE ART

Have you ever marvelled at the wonder of water? It's a liquid at room temperature, a gas when boiled and solid ice when frozen. Water is a home for many creatures, and it sustains life on earth – including ours. We drink it, cook with it and cannot survive without it. What's more, water also offers wonderful opportunities for fun, from splashing and swimming to making frozen art.

When water becomes ice it opens up a world of sparkling creativity. Trinkets from a woodland walk or a trip to the park can be suspended within coloured and frozen blocks of water to create magical ice orbs, as well as ice mobiles to hang from branches or twigs. This is an activity to spark interest both in art and in science. Budding ice artists are challenged to think about shape, size, form and even density – some things will float when placed in water and others will sink. Talking about the various containers for ice art and encouraging the sensory experience helps to deepen memory and expand vocabulary (deep/shallow; round/cube; hard/freezing; fluid/warm and so on).

The ideal time for this activity is during winter – when the weather outside mirrors the theme – making it an opportunity to learn about the seasons and to enjoy and connect with this time of the year. However, as long as you have access to a freezer, you can have a go in warmer weather, too, and talk about how melting happens more quickly in the sunshine. The end result – glistening and sparkly ice art – is a source of awe. And the transformation of liquid water to solid ice and back again is natural magic, in which themes of change can be explored. This alchemy is a joy to see.

LOCATION	Collect objects to suspend in the ice from any natural environment – woodland, fields, parks or even gardens provide endless materials. If it's cold enough (0°C/32°F overnight) you can freeze the art outside; otherwise you need a freezer.
AGE GROUP	4 years +
LEARNING ABOUT ...	Imagination ✿ curiosity ✿ creativity ✿ using the senses ✿ independence ✿ focus ✿ themes of change ✿ science ✿ communication ✿ seasonal effects
KIT	→ A small bag or container for collecting natural objects per child → Containers of various sizes, such as margarine and ice-cream tubs, Tupperware pots, oven dishes (some deep, some shallow), and so on → Water → String → Scissors → Natural food dyes → Balloons of various sizes and colours

Get ready

Talk to the children about water and how it forms ice; ask them to think about what happens to the temperature in winter. Has anyone ever seen an icicle? What does a snowflake look like? Tell them some magic will take place. They're going to collect natural items and drop them into water-filled containers, add colour to water-filled balloons – and turn it all to ice! Manage expectations about timings – they are going to create a form of sculpture that will be ready only once the water has frozen.

Show the children all the sizes of container and balloons you have and ask them to think about what sorts of items might fit inside the containers. Talk about how water expands as it freezes, so they need to leave a little bit of room at the top of each container and balloon when they pour in the water.

Get set

Let each child choose a collection bag and head off for a walk. Look for natural objects such as pine cones, twigs, evergreen needles, acorn cups, beech mast, fallen leaves, small pebbles, feathers – and anything else that the children wish to be part of their art (avoiding anything poisonous or rare).

ICE MOBILES

Go!

Fill the selected containers with water, leaving space at the top for the water to expand into as it freezes. Encourage the children to do the pouring themselves, then drop in their choice of items into each container. Get them to talk about what they notice when they drop the things into the water – they will create ripples; some will sink, others will float.

For each container, cut a piece of string that's long enough to tie to a tree branch (or wherever you plan to hang the mobile). Leave both ends of the string dangling out of the water, with the middle looped section within, to be held in place once frozen. Younger children may need help with this, but let them have a go.

Add a few drops of food dye to each container if you wish – food dye is non-toxic and easy to clean, but will run when the ice melts, so bear this in mind when thinking about where to hang the mobiles!

Put your containers outside, if it's cold enough, or in a freezer overnight.

The following day, pop the frozen mobiles out of their containers, then use the strings to hang your beautiful ice creations outside. See how the art has been captured. Watch these cool sheets of ice glisten and sparkle as they catch the light!

ICE ORBS

Go!

Put a few drops of food dye into the uninflated balloons – more drops of dye will give a stronger colour; fewer drops, a lighter colour. Some could also be left with no dye, to produce a clear orb. Pour water into the balloons. A little amount of water will make little ice orbs, and a larger amount will make larger ice orbs. Allow room for the water to expand as it freezes. Tie a knot in the end of each balloon – children may need help with this, as it can be quite fiddly trying to stop the water escaping!

TRY THIS!

> **If you want to know which colour dye is in which balloon, match the colour of the dye to the colour of the balloon (such as red dye in a red balloon, and green dye in a green balloon) – instant identification!**

Then, put the balloons in a tray and leave them to freeze overnight – outside if you can; if not, in a freezer.

The following day cut the tied ends of the balloons and peel away the rubber (always throw this away – rubber is hazardous if swallowed and does not break down). Put the ice orbs on the ground outside. Talk about how the colours have moved through the ice, how shiny they are, and how they glitter in the light.

Now watch as the ice begins to melt – if it's cold it may take a while, so talk about what might speed up the process. If the children prefer, take the orbs inside to melt.

Endings

Gather everyone to talk about the ice art – were the results what everyone was expecting? What did the children like best about the process? Which of their creations were their favourites and why?

Which ice orbs caught the light best? Which mobile melted fastest, and why?

Then, open the discussion to talk more generally about water – where do we find it? Why do we (and other animals) need it? Why do plants need it? What animals can the children think of that live in water? How do these animals 'breathe'?

Discuss the transformation of water to ice and back again. How does it happen? What do we need for freezing to happen? What do we need for melting? Consider the seasons – the passage of the sun across the sky, the shape and tilt of the earth, and how these things affect our seasons. Are seasons the same all over the world, and if not, why not? Talk about how change is a constant natural process that takes place within and around us.

TRY THIS!

If you want a more permanent piece of art, you can use the darker ice orbs to paint on paper!

BOW AND ARROW

In prehistoric times the bow and arrow was more than just a weapon to protect against attackers. It was essential for hunting food – a tool that empowered mankind for survival. Being able to craft the perfect bow or the deadliest arrowhead could mean the difference between hunger and meals for a whole tribe.

The natural world abounds with the materials for making bows and arrows: wood for the bow and the arrow shaft, stones for the arrowheads, sinew from animals for binding, resin for glue, and feathers for fletchings to stabilize the arrows in flight. Used to protect and to provide food, it's easy to see how a bow and arrow could be a precious and empowering tool to handle with respect and care, sometimes with great magical significance. Native Americans as well as the ancient Celts, for example, believed feathers represented a link between humanity and the realm of the gods – birds soaring higher than any human could go.

This energetic activity involves lots of running around! From tying knots to testing the bow, it also teaches technical skills and encourages listening, communication and problem-solving. It's an activity that requires focus, patience and determination, and when finished gives children a great sense of achievement, raising self-esteem. Tree identification, if involved, offers a connection to nature. Handling a bow and arrow also teaches about safety and responsibility. Above all, making bows and arrows is a gift for the imagination as the children leap through the ages along with the bow-wielding heroes of myth and legend, from Artemis (the Greek goddess of hunting) to Robin Hood and Peter Pan.

LOCATION	Woodland is best, but any outdoor space, such as a park or garden, with fallen sticks and enough space to run around will work.
AGE GROUP	4 years +
LEARNING ABOUT ...	Being active ❁ tree identification ❁ fine motor skills ❁ focus ❁ patience and determination ❁ achievement ❁ self-esteem ❁ safety ❁ tool use ❁ imagination ❁ language ❁ connection to nature ❁ myths and history
KIT	→ Secateurs (optional) → Penknife → Potato peeler, for stripping bark (optional) → Gardening glove → Elastic or string (elastic better if using arrows)

SAFETY FIRST

Whether an adult is using the tools alone or the children are handling them under adult supervision, follow the safety procedures described on page 60. The age at which children are able to use tools under adult supervision varies, so assess each child individually. If you are confident that the child is capable, allow tool use alone. However, close adult supervision is still required.

Get ready

Explain about the safe working zone: this is a circle the diameter of the tool user's outstretched arms. If anyone comes inside the circle, tool use should stop until the zone is empty again. Show everyone the cutting edge of the secateurs (if these are needed to cut sticks from trees) and the penknife, demonstrating how each tool works, how to position hands in order to cut safely and cleanly, how to close and lock it, and how to carry it safely (at your side, with blade pointing towards the floor, and no running!).

Show how to handle the potato peeler, holding the stick behind the peeler, with one end on the floor to stabilize it, and peeling away from the body. For extra protection, a gardening glove can be worn when using the penknife or potato peeler, but not on the hand holding the tool (as this can lessen the grip).

Stress that all tools must go back to an adult when they're no longer being used, and stored out the way with all security catches on as necessary.

Explain about the responsibility of having a toy bow and arrow, and how to play with it safely – never shoot an arrow or even aim one at another person or animal!

Get set

Head off and find your bows and arrows! For bows you are looking for sticks that are comfortable to handle, bendy and naturally crescent-shaped – hazel and young ash are ideal. For the arrows, look for short, straight sticks. Ideally, they should all come from the ground. If you have the landowner's permission to cut branches from the trees, use secateurs to make a clean cut in front of the branch bark collar or ridge, to protect the tree from damage. Older children may be responsible enough to try this under adult supervision.

TRY THIS!

Finding sticks from a particular kind of tree for the bows hones identification skills. Get the children to think about the

> different properties of trees and what might make a stick bendy or brittle.

Go!

Stripping the bow

It's time to make the bows! If the children wish, they can use the potato peeler to clean away the rough bark from the outside of the bow, making it white and smooth. Younger children can miss this step, or an adult can do it for them – encourage them to watch, and talk through the process of stripping off the bark.

Stringing the bow

Use a penknife to make a notch in the outer edge of the bow (opposite side to where the line of elastic or string will go) at the top and bottom ends of the stick. Move the penknife away from your body as you cut. Again, older children may be able to do this for themselves, under adult supervision; younger children can watch and learn.

In the notches tightly tie on a length of string or elastic, connecting one end of the stick with the other. You may need to help younger children with the tying, but encourage them to do as much as possible by first showing them and then letting them have a go. Double overhand knots will do (see section entitled "Overhand knot").

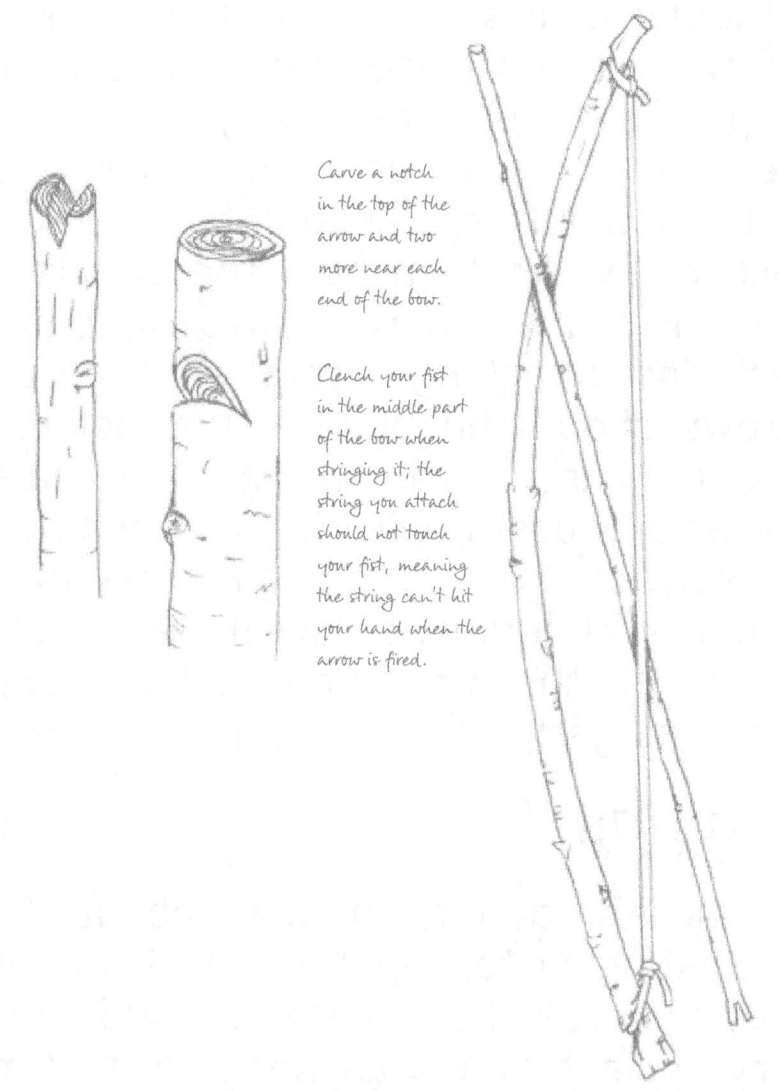

Carve a notch in the top of the arrow and two more near each end of the bow.

Clench your fist in the middle part of the bow when stringing it; the string you attach should not touch your fist, meaning the string can't hit your hand when the arrow is fired.

Making arrows

Younger children with their imagination fired may be happy at this stage to run around with the bows, without arrows. If you are making arrows, a potato peeler can be used to strip away the outer bark, smoothing the arrow sticks. Use the penknife to make a notch across the back end of each arrow, to help hold the elastic or string in place when the arrow is pulled back for launching. Front ends of the arrows should be blunt – not pointed! Targets ensure the firing is focused (especially useful with large groups).

Now let the games begin! Encourage delighted cheers when an archer's arrow soars into the air – and perhaps even hits a target!

Endings

There's a lot to say about the fascinating history of bows and arrows! They were used all over the world, from very ancient times, as weapons and for hunting. Some of the earliest arrowheads, found in South Africa, date back an incredible 64,000 years! In some regions, such as tribal areas of the Americas, the use of the bow and arrow as a primary weapon lasted as late as the 19th century, and some indigenous peoples still use them today. In Europe, the decline in use of the bow and arrow as a weapon in the 16th century gave rise to the sport of archery, which is now part of the Olympic Games.

Explain the terms associated with bows and arrows – does anyone know what a person who makes bows and arrows is called? (A fletcher.) Does anyone know what you'd use a quiver for? (Carrying the arrows.)

Who knows what the earliest bows and arrows were made from (see section entitled "BOW AND ARROW")? What aspects of the bow's shape and form make it brilliant for launching an arrow? What features of an arrow make it good at flying through the air? Can anyone say which trees provide the bendiest sticks and which ones the straightest arrows?

What do the children like about their bow and arrow? Is there anything they would add to it – if so, why?

WOODLAND JEWELLERY

Collecting natural objects and using them in different ways to adorn our bodies is a practice that stretches back into ancient history. Jewellery made from shells, stones

and even bones has survived from prehistoric times. For example, some beads found in a cave in Israel, made from the shell of the sea snail *(Nassarius)* , are thought to be 90,000–100,000 years old. And even older is a necklace of eagle talons dating back an incredible 130,000 years – making this activity one of our earliest pastimes!

Children seem to tap straight into this age-old art when they craft their own pieces of jewellery. No gold or gemstones are needed, only a few pieces of wood and a handful of decorations from the forest floor, along with string and some simple tools. This is a very creative activity that brings on a truly meditative atmosphere in which children can lose themselves, experiencing deep focus and really paying attention to detail as they explore and engage with colour, shape and texture.

The whole process of cutting, drilling and stringing together the carefully crafted parts of a necklace or bracelet builds patience and perseverance, and helps to develop fine motor skills as well as mathematical understanding (through working with three-dimensional shapes). It also teaches about safe risk-taking through handling tools correctly and responsibly, whether the tools are used or only observed in use.

LOCATION	Woodland is ideal as it provides the natural materials for the jewellery, and large logs and stumps offer useful working surfaces. However, if you have already collected the materials, any outdoor location will do.
AGE GROUP	4 years +
LEARNING ABOUT ...	Focus ✿ persistence ✿ patience ✿ creativity ✿ using fine motor skills ✿ risk assessment (using tools responsibly) ✿ using the senses ✿ confidence ✿ tree identification

SAFETY FIRST

All these activities involve using cutting or drilling tools. Whether an adult is using the tools alone or the children are handling them under adult supervision, follow the safety procedures. The age at which children are able to use tools under adult supervision varies, so assess each child individually. If you are confident that the child is capable, allow tool use alone. However, close adult supervision is still required.

Most importantly, designing and crafting a unique piece of woodland jewellery brings with it a real sense of pride and self-esteem!

ELDER-BEAD NECKLACE OR BRACELET

KIT	→ Gardening gloves for children who will be using tools or assisting others → Small secateurs → Straight knitting needles in small (3mm), medium (7mm) and large (10mm) sizes (or use sturdy twigs – safer for young children) → String → Scissors
OPTIONAL	Decorative art materials, such as paintbrushes, child-friendly acrylic paint, paint tray, permanent marker pens, etc.

Get ready get

Find some elder *(Sambucus)* bushes. Elder is especially good for making beads for jewellery, as in spring and summer the pith (centre tissue) of the stems is soft, spongy and easy to poke out.

Choose stems of the right size (you should get the landowner's permission before cutting any stems). If making bracelets, they need to be big enough for the small knitting needle to pass through (remember that string will pass through this hole too). For necklaces, look for stems that are big enough for the larger needles to go through. If you don't want to use knitting needles to poke out the pith, gather some sturdy twigs of about the equivalent size.

Get set

Talk about the safe working zone and safe tool use (see section entitled "Get set"). Show everyone the cutting edge of the secateurs, demonstrating how they work and how to close and lock them.

Use the secateurs to cut a stem. Make a clean cut, without tearing the bark, to protect the tree from damage. Capable children can try this themselves under adult supervision, keeping their free hand (the hand without the tool) at least a hand's width away from the cutting edge. For extra safety, they can wear a glove on their free hand (not on their tool hand as this can lessen the grip), but some may find it easier to hold the secateurs with two hands to cut the stems.

Go!

Cutting

Now start creating the jewellery. Decide how many beads you want and use the secateurs to cut the stem into bead lengths. About 2.5cm (1in) – roughly the distance from the tip of an adult's thumb to their knuckle – works well, but play around with the bead length if you like. Children can try to do this themselves (under supervision), following the safety steps above. Adults should assist the younger ones where necessary. Remind the children to lock the secateurs and hand them back to an adult once they've finished with them.

Around 2.5cm (1in) is a good bead size, but try out different lengths.

Poking

Use a knitting needle or sturdy twig (safer for younger children) to poke out the pith. All poking should be done away from the body, never toward it or down toward the knees.

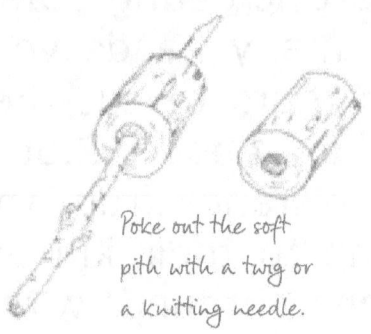

Poke out the soft pith with a twig or a knitting needle.

Decorating and stringing

Now you have your beads. They can be decorated with marker pens or paints (if you don't want to spend time in the woods decorating all the beads, do this stage at home, once the jewellery has been strung).

Finally, it's time to string the beads! Cut a piece of string that's long enough to go over a head or hand, with a little left over for knotting. Once all the beads are in place, tie the two ends of the string together using an overhand knot (see section entitled "Overhand knot").

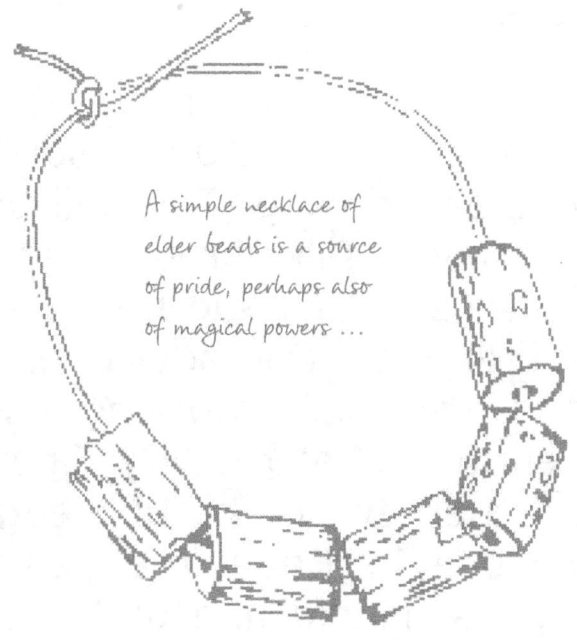

A simple necklace of elder beads is a source of pride, perhaps also of magical powers ...

Now wear the woodland jewels with pride!

WOOD COOKIE NECKLACE

KIT	→ Gardening gloves for each adult and for any children doing cutting/drilling → Hand-held folding saw → Palm drill → String → Scissors
OPTIONAL	Decorative art materials, such as charcoal, oil-based pastels, permanent marker pens, etc.

Get ready

Look for a large fallen tree trunk or sturdy stump, to provide a solid prop for sawing and drilling. This will become your workspace. Talk through the safety aspects of using a hand-held saw and a palm drill (see the advice on using tools and the safe working zone in section entitled "Get ready"). Show how to unfold the saw, its cutting edge and how to close it. Show the palm drill, indicating its handle and drill bit.

Find a reasonably knot-and rot-free branch, roughly as long as an adult's arm and about 5–6cm (2–2½in) in diameter. Use a fallen branch, if possible. If cutting from a tree, you'll need the landowner's permission, and be sure to make a clean cut in front of the branch bark collar or ridge to protect the tree from damage. It's usually the adult who cuts the branch and assesses if it will supply enough wood cookies for the group, gathering an extra branch if necessary.

Get set

Demonstrate how to cut a wood cookie. Prop the branch up against the log or tree stump. Kneel down in front of the branch (this is a steady position that ensures all limbs are out harm's way). Put a gardening glove on your free (non-cutting) hand and use this hand (and if necessary your knee) to hold still the lower side of the branch – the end that is not being cut). Your free hand (the non-cutting hand) should be roughly 15cm (6in) away from the cutting edge. Saw off the end of the branch to create a clean, flat surface. Then move your saw 1.5–2cm (½–¾in) along the branch and cut off another section: this disc is your wood cookie!

Move the branch out of the way and put the disc on top of the supportive surface. Hold the wooden disc still with your gloved hand and use the palm drill to make a hole through the cookie, close to the edge.

Go!

Sawing

Now the demonstration is over, it's time for the kids to have a go! If you are working with a ratio of one adult to one child, the adult in the pair braces and secures the branch; and the child kneels down, takes hold of the saw handle with both their hands and saws off their cookie. If there are more children split them into pairs, kneeling down and facing each other, to brace and steady the branch while a third child cuts a cookie. Once this is done, they switch roles so another child can cut a cookie. An adult must supervise each pair, helping to brace too, if necessary. If anyone seems to be struggling, ask if they need help.

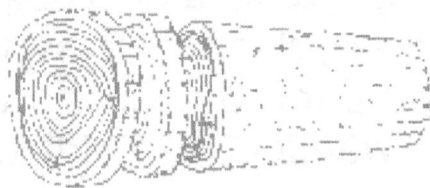

One fallen branch can yield enough wood cookies for a whole group, so long as it is dry and rot-free.

Drilling

An adult needs to hold the cookie steady in a gloved hand as the child uses the palm drill to bore a hole near the edge. If older children feel they would like to try this alone, holding their own cookie as they drill, let them have a go but under very close adult supervision. Once the discs are ready, put the tools away safely.

Decorating and stringing

Now it's time to start turning the wood cookies into pendants by drawing or painting on pictures, symbols or patterns – whatever inspires the children. Characters from the ancient Ogham alphabet (see section entitled "MAGIC WANDS"), many of which represent trees, make great decorations. (If there's any danger of materials staining clothes, decorate one side of the cookie only.) When the designs are finished, thread a length of string through the hole in the wooden disc, then tie the ends with an overhand knot (see section entitled "Overhand knot"). Make sure the string is long enough to go easily over the head when tied.

ACORN PENDANT

KIT	→ Gardening gloves for adults and any children using tools → 2.5mm auger gimlet (or a selection of sizes if possible – acorns can vary in size) → Wool needle smaller in diameter than the auger gimlet drill bit → Permanent marker pens (ideally one per child) → Lengths of string or differently coloured wool (thin enough to fit through the drilled hole) → Scissors
OPTIONAL	Decorative art materials, such as oil-based pastels, permanent marker pens

Get ready

If you are in woodland, find a large fallen tree trunk or sturdy stump, for resting the acorn on while drilling the hole. Collect the acorns, at least two per person. The larger ones will be easier to handle.

Get set

Show everyone the auger – indicating its handle and its screwdriver-like drill bit. Remind everyone about the importance of using tools safely and about the safe working zone (see section entitled "Get set"). Demonstrate how to use the auger to drill a hole through the acorn, from side to side, by pressing and twisting the drill through the acorn just beneath its cap.

GO!

Drilling

Each child rests their acorn on a solid surface, such as a big log or tree stump. Get them to put a glove on the hand holding the acorn, but not on the other one. Watch carefully as they drill a hole through the acorn from side to side as you've demonstrated, offering advice and support as necessary. The acorn can split if they drill too vigorously – they'll need to apply steady but gentle pressure and take their time. No problem if the acorn splits – that's what the spare acorn is for!

Let younger children do as much as they can, perhaps helping by starting the hole off for them or assisting throughout the whole process. Remind everyone about putting tools away safely after use.

Decorating and stringing

Once everyone has at least one acorn with a drilled hole, it's time to use a marker pen to draw on a funny face, or a pattern such as spots, or anything else that comes to mind. Let each child choose a length of string or coloured wool. Thread the string or wool through each acorn, checking it's long enough to fit over the head when tied. If it's difficult to get it through the hole, poke or thread it onto the wool needle and push it through (this is great for hand–eye co-ordination!) Once the string or wool is threaded through, pull it to even up the loose ends, then use an overhand knot (see section entitled "Overhand knot") to tie them together. Now everyone has an acorn friend to wear around their neck!

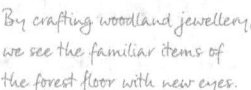

By crafting woodland jewellery, we see the familiar items of the forest floor with new eyes.

Endings

Now's the time to admire each other's handiwork. Talk about all the designs the children have chosen and ask them to explain what they love best about their jewellery. What did they enjoy most about the activity, and what did they find tricky? Can anyone think of any other natural materials for 'jewels'? For example, beads can be made from clay, shells, coral, seeds or stone. As well as acorns, are there any other nuts that could be used?

You could broaden your discussion to consider how jewellery has been used throughout history. From sparkling crystals and stones as blue as the sky to golden hair pins and engraved belt buckles, jewellery has both ornamental and functional uses. Does it mark a person's social status, like the crown of a queen? Or does it protect the wearer or give them special power? Ancient Egyptian amulets were often shaped like animal gods, imbuing the wearer with the gods' attributes, or bore inscriptions that transferred the magical powers they represented to the person wearing them.

Talk about using natural materials sensitively when making jewellery, only collecting what you need. Try not to take branches that have flowers or berries on them, as these provide food for wildlife and the seeds of future trees. Look first to the forest floor for ideas for decorations.

STICK FRAMES

A stick frame has so many different uses. It can capture an experience in nature, with all the connected memories, ideas and feelings – perhaps by framing a photograph taken on a country walk, or a collage of leaves collected along the way, or a drawing of a favourite flower. Alternatively, placed on the ground, a stick frame displays in a living picture the amazing richness of mini-beast and plant life in one small patch of earth.

Children can use string to weave a spider's web across the frame, working from edge to edge and seeing for themselves the industry, patience and logic it takes for the humble spider to build a trap for its prey. Or a stick frame may become a decoration for a den, the visible effects of weathering and time offering a chance to learn about the processes of change and decay.

Creating a stick frame teaches about angles and knot tying, developing fine motor skills. It promotes patience, focus and perseverance. Once it's made, well-earned success and new skills raise self-esteem. Whatever the size of the group, talking through ideas and sharing tips builds trust, empathy, pride and teamwork. And this frame also offers a great way to capture memories!

Get ready

Gather the sticks – four per frame. Sticks can be any length, so long as the frame-makers can handle them. They should be sturdy and rot-free, but whether they're twisted and bumpy or smooth and straight is up to the frame-makers.

Get set

Ask the children to think about what they might use their frame for. If it's for a picture, what will the picture be of and how will they create it? With leaves and other found items? With paper, paints or pencils? If they want to frame a picture of life on the ground, ask them to consider what sort of area might provide the greatest number of plants and insects to discover. What will help them make the best observations – long grass, short grass, a woodland floor, or a mixture of these?

LOCATION	Any natural outdoor setting, ideally a woodland with fallen sticks
AGE GROUP	4 years +
LEARNING ABOUT ...	Ecology ⊛ creativity ⊛ imagination ⊛ focus ⊛ confidence ⊛ independence ⊛ self-esteem ⊛ maths ⊛ connecting with nature
KIT	→ 4 sticks per person, if suitable fallen ones are not available on the ground → String → Scissors → Art materials (paper, cloth, colouring pencils, paints, sticky tape, wool and so on – optional) → Coloured wool (optional)

Go!

To bind each frame, cut roughly an adult's arm-length of string for each of the frame's four corners.

Lay the end of one stick across the top of another at a 90-degree angle, leaving about 2.5cm (1in) sticking out to form the arms of a cross. Take your string underneath the vertical stick at the bottom of this cross and tie a double overhand knot (see section entitled "Overhand knot").

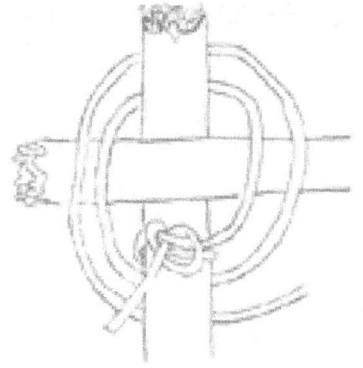

Weave the string several times up and over the crossed sticks.

It can help to think of the crossed sticks as a compass, with north, south, east and west bearings. Bring the long end of the string up and over the east side of the horizontal stick and then under the north side of the vertical stick, then again over the west side of the horizontal stick, and under the south side of the vertical stick. Repeat this pattern five or six times pulling tightly at each turn to fix the sticks in place, finishing with a double overhand knot. Cut any excess string away. One section of your frame is now securely fastened. This sort of binding is known by the term 'square lashing', which refers to the 90° angle (square corner) the binding creates on the sticks.

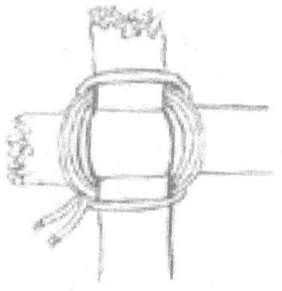

Once pulled tight, the square lashing holds each corner securely in place.

Lay down the secured sticks in their original positions. Now take another stick and position it as the opposite vertical side to the first stick (creating the right-hand side of the square), making a cross in the corner as before. Using the same tying and lashing method, bind on the third stick. Finally, position the last stick across the bottom of the square, attaching it at one end first, and then at the other to make a full, square frame. Success!

Once the frames are made, it's time to create a beautiful artwork to go inside, or to position them over a patch of earth for an ecological study, or to weave coloured wool in a spider's web over the frame or to use it in some other innovative way!

Endings

Talk about each frame and what it has become – lavish praise and admiration on these works of art, each unique. If a patch of ground was framed what did the children see? Talk about how the weather and seasons might change how this particular segment of land looks.

TRY THIS!

With two longer sticks, you can make a rectangular frame. With three sticks of equal length, you can make a triangular frame. Be creative!

It's interesting to consider what will happen to the frames if they're left outside. They will eventually break down, providing nutrients for the growth of other species. This decay is a vital function of a healthy ecosystem – a natural part of our earth's cycles.

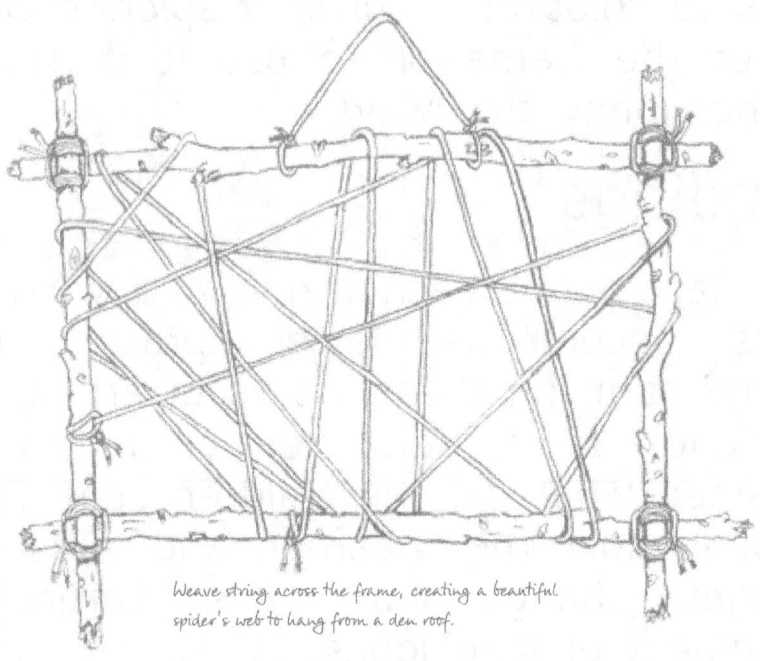

Weave string across the frame, creating a beautiful spider's web to hang from a den roof.

What can the children tell you about the sticks they've found? Are they bendy or brittle? What does that say about the sticks? Does anyone know what trees the sticks may have come from? You could talk about different tree species in your local area and how to identify them.

What did the children love most about making the frames? Did they find anything difficult, like the knot-tying?

Maybe they would like to practise tying knots again to master this new skill?

Survival Skills

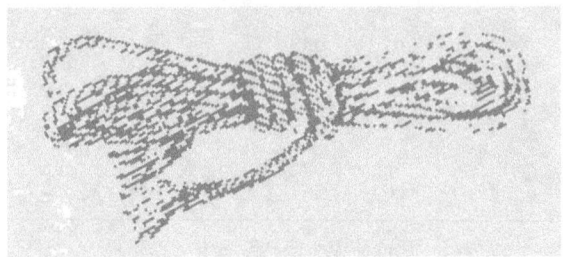

Despite all the modern conveniences and digital distractions of the 21st century, children still love learning the basic skills of survival: how to build a shelter, light a fire and gather food from the wild. For many of us, our connection to natural spaces has become more limited for a multitude of reasons, but this doesn't seem to have weakened the immediate link today's children seem to have with these ancient activities when they are given the opportunity to experience them.

The activities in this chapter can give children a lasting increase in self-confidence, self-esteem and independence. There is so much to learn in the woods. To build a den with friends, for example, using the materials available on the forest floor, takes resourcefulness, concentration, persistence and communication, as well as problem-solving skills. Fire lighting encourages each child to take part in assessing risks and thinking about how to reduce them.

When children draw on their inner resources to meet their own basic needs, they connect directly with the natural world around them, and find a sense of belonging, a special place. And that's when a shelter in the wilderness becomes a home.

ESSENTIAL KNOTS

It's hard to say when people first began tying knots because the earliest cord would have been made of organic material (hair, sinew, plant fibre) that has long since decomposed. However, archaeological evidence such as holed beads and wear marks on artefacts suggests that knots were used as far back as the Pleistocene period, the time of ice ages and woolly mammoths (2.5 million to 11,700 years ago). And the use of knots could well be even more ancient than this.

Knots have been essential to human development for a multitude of reasons. In prehistoric times they were used to make spears and traps for capturing food. The Egyptians needed them to haul giant stones to make the great pyramids. They have been used to make bridges and baskets, to build shelters and fasten clothes. Seamanship manuals of the 1700s survive, with descriptions of elaborate knots used for hoisting sails, anchoring ships and trawling with fishing nets. Knots have a cultural and spiritual aspect, too, such as those found in the mosaics of the Roman and medieval eras, Celtic designs and Chinese folk art.

> ### TRY THIS!
> **Practise at home using pieces of string around chair legs or your own foot.**

Whether knots are being used in art, for putting up shelters or for tying your shoelaces, their skill, beauty and practicality are still important to us today. Knot tying develops fine motor skills, concentration, memory and persistence, and fills those who master each new knot with a sense of confidence, independence and self-reliance. This is a skill that helps children think about the concepts of mathematics and physics, and it is one that can be shared, nurturing a sense of community and teamwork.

Once you are familiar with the knots in section entitled "ESSENTIAL KNOTS", you can use them to tie together woodland jewellery, set up a tarpaulin shelter or in any number of other ways. We love to use quick-release knots. As the name suggests, they are speedy to put up and untie, which is ideal if you need to put up a tarp fast in rainy weather! Our favoured ones are the Siberian hitch and the Cawley hitch. Aged four, our son took naturally to the overhand knot and the timber hitch. His bursting pride at his newfound skill was a true joy to witness! Knots are fantastic fun. Enjoy them, master them and find out which ones are yours.

LOCATION	Anywhere you need a knot!
AGE GROUP	4 years +
LEARNING ABOUT ...	Memory ✣ concentration ✣ persistence ✣ fine motor skills ✣ confidence ✣ self-reliance ✣ independence ✣ teamwork ✣ mathematics ✣ physics
KIT	Paracord: 50–100m (165–330ft) spool. Our preferred cord for knots is paracord, as it is strong, easy to untie and comes in various colours, but feel free to play around with different materials, such as bank line, outdoor rope, utility cord and string (good for woodland jewellery). A 50–100m (165–330ft) spool will allow you to cut to length as required. (The amount needed for a tarpaulin set-up, for example, will vary depending on size of trees, spacing, etc.)

Overhand knot

Probably the simplest and best-known knot is the overhand knot. Tied in a single piece of cord, it can act as a stopper to prevent something slipping off or to help prevent fraying.

Choose your required length of cord and make a loop in the end. Tuck the short end through the loop and pull tight.

Overhand knot for jewellery

This knot is great for tying two ends of cord securely together, making a fixed loop. It has a huge range of uses, such as creating a necklace or bracelet, hanging a pocket knife from a belt and suspending a cooking pot above a fire.

The steps are the same as above but this time line up both ends of your cord and make a loop with the doubled-up cord. Thread the free ends through the loop and pull tight, to create a fixed loop of the desired size.

TARP RIDGELINE KNOTS

The ridgeline is the cord, rope or string line that your tarpaulin will hang over. This line needs to be taut so the tarp it supports provides the desired secure, dry shelter. To make the ridgeline taut you will need to tie it around two supporting trees (or other structures) using knots to anchor and tension the ends securely in place. Choose your anchoring and tensioning knots from the examples below.

Anchoring knots

Slip knot

Make a loop in your line, then make another one next to the first loop **(1)**.

Pull the second loop through the first one **(2),** tightening to create a single fixed loop **(3).**

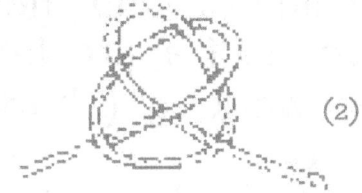

Holding the fixed loop in one hand, wrap the line around the supporting tree (or other chosen structure), thread the free end through the loop and pull to tighten the knot **(4).**

To undo the slip knot, work the free end back through the loop and pull the cord either side of the knot.

(4)

Timber hitch

Take your line around the supporting tree, giving yourself approximately 90cm (35in) at the working (shorter) end to make your knot.

Pass the shorter working end over the longer end of your cord, then bring the working end underneath the non-working (longer) end and thread the working end over itself and through the middle of the loop created around the tree **(1).**

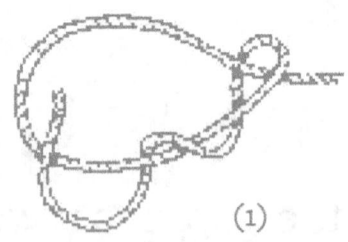

(1)

Keep looping the short end around the loop, 3–4 times more. Pull and tighten the knot against the tree **(2).**

To release, slacken the line and unloop the knot.

(2)

Siberian hitch

Take your line around the supporting tree, giving yourself at least 90cm (35in) at the working (shorter) end to make your knot. Place the lines in your palm, with your thumb next to the non-working (longer) end of your cord **(1)**.

Take the working end of your cord and wrap it under and around your fingers once. Now hold both ends of the line with your free (unwrapped) hand **(2)**.

Point your wrapped fingers down toward the ground. Then, keeping all the cord on your palm side, bring your wrapped fingers up toward the sky (your thumb should eventually be vertical in front of and facing your chest) **(3).**

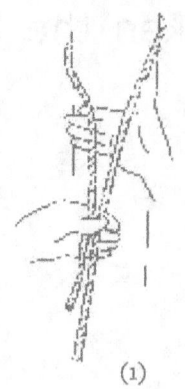

(1)

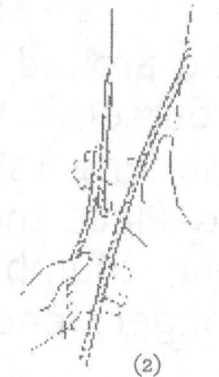

(2)

(3)

(4)

Roll your wrapped fingers across the top of the lines and grab the working line **(4)**.

Wiggle your wrapped fingers free and let the loop around these fingers slip off while you pull the working end through it. Do not, however, pull the working line all the way through this loop. The working line that you pulled through should now also form a loop **(5)**.

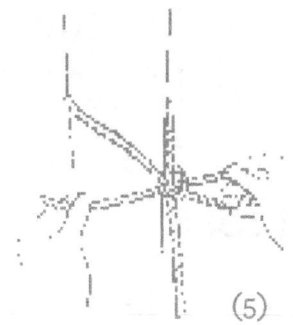
(5)

Hold the non-working end of the line with your free hand and use your other hand to push the knot up against the tree, anchoring it in place **(6)**.

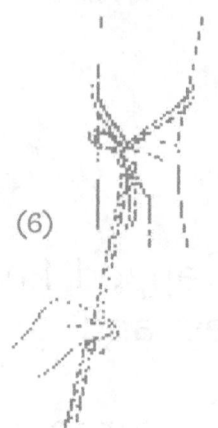

This is a quick-release knot, so you simply pull on the working (shorter) end of the line when you need to untie it.

Tensioning knots

Once your anchoring knot is in place, a tensioning knot at the other end of the line, at the second tree, ensures e is taut. Here are some examples:

Cawley hitch

Wrap your line around the supporting tree, leaving at least 60cm (24in) to make the knot. Pass the working end under the ridgeline and wrap it around the ridgeline 3–4 times working toward the tree **(1)**.

The next time pass the working end over both sections of cord, creating a hole to pull the working end through. Pull the working end through, but not all the way, to form a loop. Pull this loop tight to finish the knot **(2)**.

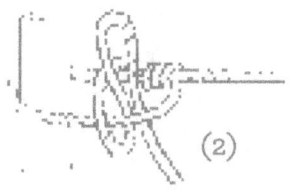

The coil you created can slide up and down the will also grip onto the ridgeline wherever you leave it, to make the ridgeline taut. To undo this quick-release knot, simply pull on the loose end.

TRY THIS!

> **The Siberian hitch and Cawley hitch are both good for tying your tarp to Take your line ground pegs.**

Taut tarp hitch

Take your line around the tree, leaving enough cord to wrap it a second time around the tree and at least 90cm (35in) to make your knot. Pull tightly on the working end to tension the ridgeline **(1)**.

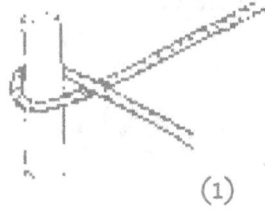

(1)

Keep the tension on and wrap the working end across the top of the ridgeline. Pull back, away from the ridgeline, and wrap the working end of the line around the back of the tree. This will begin to tension the line **(2)**.

Now pass the working end across the top of the ridgeline, to make a triangle shape **(3)**.

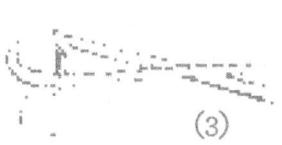

Inside the triangle, pull the working end through to form a loop (or half hitch). Pull on this to tighten the line against the tree **(4)**.

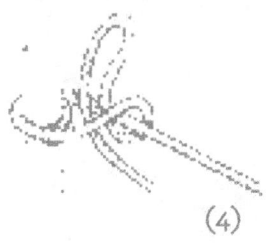

To secure it in place, pull the working end through the first loop to form another loop, and tighten **(5)**.

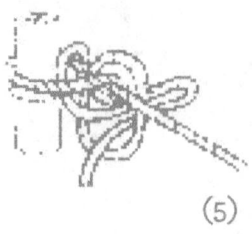

(5)

To undo this quick-release knot, simply pull the loose end.

Prusik knot

Also used in climbing, this friction knot will slide along and grip onto another line, staying in its final position. To tighten up and hold in place a tarp along a ridgeline, use the Prusik knot as follows:

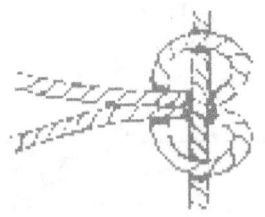

Take a 30cm (12in) piece of cord and line up the ends. Place the looped end under the ridgeline, pull it up and wrap it around the ridgeline by threading the loose ends through the loop.

Wrap it under and around the ridgeline again. Do this 3-4 times, keeping each turn neatly lined up against each other.

On the final wrap pass the free ends of the cord back through the loop and pull tight. The Prusik knot is now in place.

You could use a simple overhand knot (see section entitled "Overhand knot") to tie the loose ends to your tarp eyelets. Pull the tarp taut and leave in place. To undo, loosen the tension and unwind the knots.

BUILDING SHELTERS

'Shelter' means so many different things: protection from the elements, safety, a hideout, a sanctuary, a place to get together, a home. Throughout history humans have made shelters to meet their basic needs, and even today children still have a natural instinct to build them, starting with those dens at home made from chairs, sheets and pillows.

A shelter in the woods is a child's home in nature, separate from the adult world. It feels like a place of their own, somewhere they belong, and this sense of connection is deepened as they return to a certain spot to build there again. We can't count how many times children have pulled us along to see what they've made, bursting with pride! A few basic skills are all that's needed to create a huge range of shelters, and as for natural decoration the options are unlimited, from hanging flowers and stick mailboxes to pretend log fires in a ring of pebbles and cosy beds of leaves.

This is a healthy, energetic activity, and one that gives children a chance to assess potential risks and take actions to lessen them, so gaining a sense of responsibility. By thinking about ground conditions, the types of branches they can use, the trees that make good supports, the effects of the elements, the children connect closely with the natural world. Working out which length of branch or cord to use, and who will place it and where, helps to develop mathematics, communication and listening skills and teamwork. Even architecture is touched upon, as the children design their structure and make it secure. And when the shelter is complete, they gain an incredible feeling of achievement, self-reliance and confidence in their own abilities; and from sharing this unique space comes a sense of empathy and community.

LOCATION	Woodland, where trees, branches and leaves are readily available, is the perfect location. However, tarps can also be placed in gardens or parks with suitable tree cover or indeed elsewhere outdoors if appropriate supports can be found.
AGE GROUP	3 years + (starting with mini shelters)
LEARNING ABOUT ...	Being active ✲ responsibility ✲ managing risk ✲ self-reliance ✲ achievement ✲ connecting with nature ✲ mathematics ✲ language ✲ teamwork ✲ listening skills ✲ architecture ✲ empathy
KIT	For woodland shelters and mini shelters you need only what nature supplies and perhaps gardening gloves. For tarpaulin shelters, you will need: → A tarpaulin, size dependent on the number of people using the shelter. Tarps come in different materials, such as plastic or coated waterproof fabrics like DD tarps (our preference as they are versatile, soft and light) and in many colours (including camouflage). Some have guylines and pegs. → Paracord of a length suitable for your current and future use (see page 83) → 4 tent pegs (for tent-shaped shelter) → Scissors → Rubber hammer (optional) → Gardening gloves for those doing hammering (optional) → Groundsheet and/or blanket (optional)

Some suggestions for building shelters are offered on the next pages, but really all you need to do is teach children the basic skills and safe working techniques. Then the mere suggestion of going shelter building will unfold naturally into incredible creativity and inventiveness. This is a fantastic transforming activity and a wonderful way to share in the magic of nature.

TARPAULIN SHELTERS

Get ready

To make a tent-shaped shelter, the tarp will be hung over a paracord ridgeline suspended between two trees (creating an upside-down V). When you've found two trees growing reasonably close together, everyone can check that they are both healthy and suitable for supporting the shelter. Look at the trunk: is it intact or does it have fungus growing from it, which indicates disease?

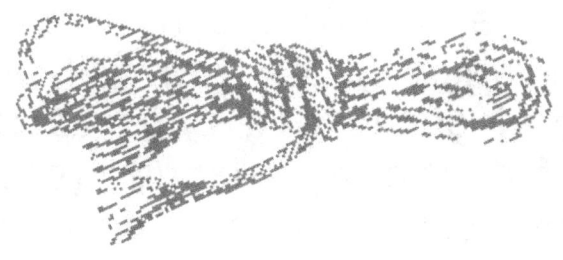

Look up: are there any dead or diseased hanging branches that could fall onto the shelter? Ideally, you also want a flat ground surface that is not too hard, as this is where you will sit and put the pegs. Also check the ground for rubbish, trip hazards and ant nests!

Get set

Once you've found the best spot, show everyone how the tarp, cord and pegs work together, with the cord going through the tarp's eyelets to secure the shelter along the ridgeline and at ground level, with the help of pegs.

Then it's time to design the space. Do you want a tent-shaped shelter with the sides at ground level or something that's more like a roof, higher up the tree? Decide before you start building so you know where to put your ridgeline and how much cord to use. Choose which knots you will be using for the ridgeline and pegs as this will also affect the cord length (see below and the selection of anchoring and tensioning knots in section entitled "Anchoring knots & Tensioning knots"). Cord can be tough to cut, so an adult may need to demonstrate this first, offering assistance if needed. Prevent cut cord from fraying by tying an overhand knot (see section entitled "Overhand knot") at each end.

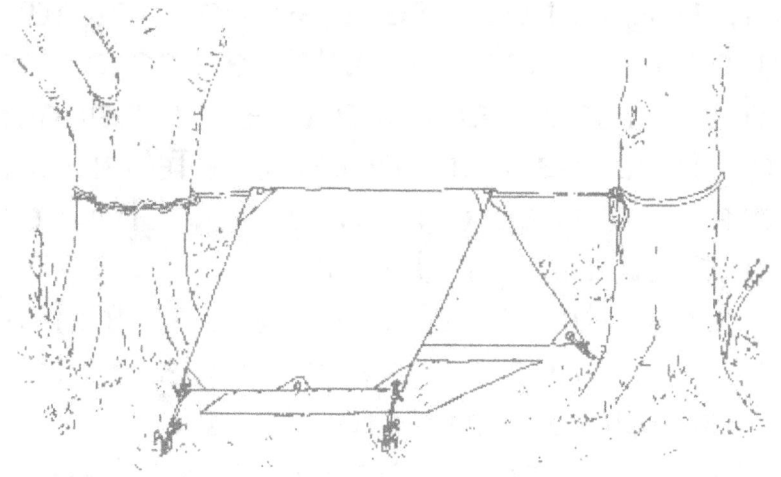

TRY THIS!

A tall branch can be used to make the tarp stand up in the middle, with the edges pegged down like a marquee (cut the top of the branch flat and remove twigs to prevent ripping). Or try using the tarpaulin as a flat roof tied to four trees (if rain is likely, position one side higher to help the water run off).

Go!

The shelter-building begins! Attach the ridgeline to the first tree, using an anchoring knot (see section entitled "Anchoring knots"). Pull the line across to the second tree, and use a tensioning knot (see section entitled "Tensioning knots") to secure it in place. The cord should be nice and taut.

Hang the tarp over the ridgeline, even it up and secure it in place along the ridgeline with one Prusik knot at either end (see section entitled "Prusik knot") – you may need to cut two 30cm (12in) lengths of cord if your tarp did not come with guylines for tensioning. You'll also need to cut four suitable lengths of cord for your pegs (if guylines did not come with the tarp). Peg the four corners of the tarp to the ground using your chosen knots; for example, a jewellery overhand knot looped through the eyelet and around the peg, or a Siberian hitch attached to the tarp eyelet with a Cawley hitch looped around the peg. The leader should demonstrate how to push in the pegs safely using a rubber hammer, and explain about the safe working zone during tool use (see section entitled "Get ready"). Wear a glove on the hand that will hold the peg, but never on the hand holding the hammer as gloves can make it can slip. Kneel down when hammering so you are stable, keeping your knees and feet out of the way. With fairly soft ground there is no need to whack the peg – small taps should be enough. Never raise the hammer above your head.

To help prevent the pegs slipping out when the tarp is tied in place, hammer in the pegs at an angle, with the hook end facing away from the tarp. Allow children to have a go under positive supervision and offer assistance to those that may need it. However, a hammer may not be needed – if the ground is fairly soft, a sturdy log or even just feet in boots can be used to push in the pegs.

If you have a groundsheet or blanket, this can now go underneath the tarp. Now the shelter can be decorated to make it really stand out, or maybe just left to blend in with its surroundings.

WOODLAND SHELTERS

There are many ways to build a woodland shelter, depending on the tree types available and the fallen branches and leaves you find on the forest floor. A couple of ideas are suggested here, but feel free to experiment. It's great fun – just make sure the shelters are sturdy and secure. It's a good idea to check with the landowner if the shelter needs to be dismantled afterwards or if certain tree species should be avoided. Try to leave the environment as you found it.

Get ready

You can wear gardening gloves to protect your hands. For ease and to help avoid injury to yourself and others, hold any branches by the trunk end and trail them along the ground behind you. And keep an eye open for trip hazards! When assessing suitable trees, remember to look up and check that they are free of disease and any overhanging dead branches (see section entitled "TARPAULIN SHELTERS: Get ready").

Survey the terrain and decide if you want to make a tent-shaped shelter or a tepee-shaped one.

Get set

To make a tent-shaped shelter from woodland materials, you need two nearby trees with Y-shaped trunks or protruding limbs to support a branch between them. You also need a sturdy branch that is long enough to reach through both trees and strong enough to support many smaller branches. For a tepee shelter, you'll need a large tree as a central support.

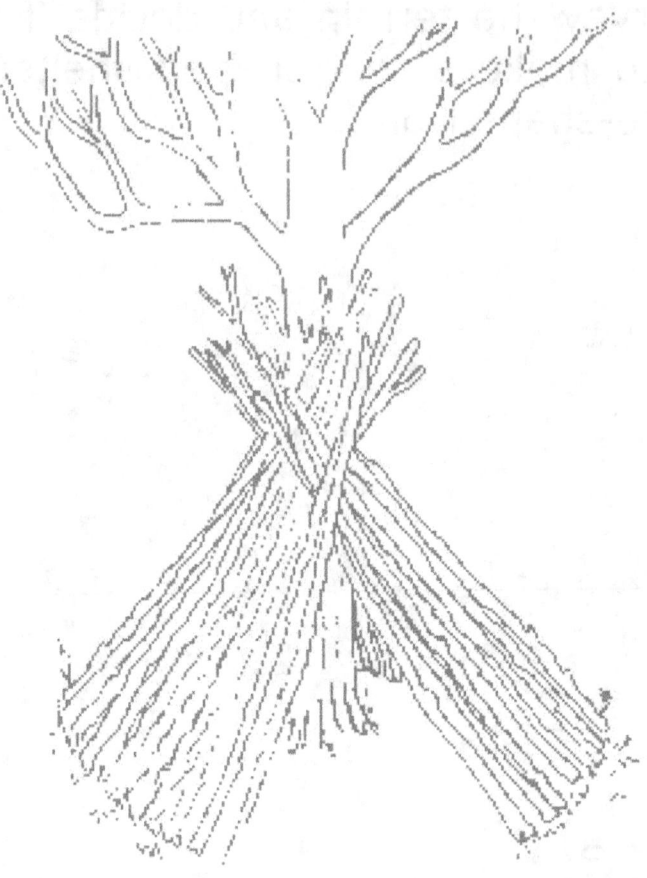

Go!

For a tent-shaped shelter, place the branch in the Y-shaped notches, checking it's secure and sturdy. Now collect as many smaller branches as possible and lean them at an angle against both sides of the supporting branch to form the walls and roof. Leave a small section uncovered, to be your entrance. Pack fallen leaves into the roof and walls, to help make the shelter cosy and waterproof.

For a tepee shelter, gather long branches and lean them at angles in a circle around the central supporting tree, leaving a space for the door. Secure the branches in place by pushing them into the earth or piling logs around their base. To fill in gaps, gather up smaller, bendy sticks and prop them against the larger branches or weave them in-between. If you wish to, fill in the walls with gathered leaves.

> ### TRY THIS!
> **If trees with Y-shaped notches cannot be found, a lean-to shelter can be made against a long horizontal branch, a fallen tree or some other natural structure. See what you can find!**

Now stand back, take in the view and enter! This is your shelter. Will you put leaves on the floor as carpet and make a pretend fire for warmth? Or will this become a camouflaged hideout, a quiet place to spy on wildlife passing by? Or something else?

MINI SHELTERS

This is a wonderful activity for younger children, who may not be big enough to help build a full-size den. It's also a great opportunity to model new shelter ideas before putting them into practice.

> ### TRY THIS!
> **For a free-standing tepee, lay three long branches together on the ground and tie them together about 30cm (12in) from the top. Stand them up and pull them apart to create a tripod, digging the bottom branch ends into the ground. Then weave other branches through this frame.**

Get ready

Ask who this special little shelter is for. It could be for a doll or a teddy, for fairies, for bugs or to house mini mud faces (see section entitled "MUD FACES") or clay people – the choices are endless!

Get set

Look for the perfect place to build the shelter, perhaps against a tree or a log.

Go!

Gather up all the sticks you need, make sure they are large enough to shelter who it's intended for and prop them against your chosen support. The shelter is now ready for your special guest!

Endings

There are lots of things the children might like to talk about afterwards. What did they like best about their shelter, and why? If they built one again, would it be the same or different? Did they prefer any of the knots, and why? You could talk about the types of shelters our ancestors might have used at different times of year, perhaps caves in winter and woodland structures in summer – and maybe they even used similar methods to these ones!

What other natural materials could people use to build shelters, and what might affect their choice? Think about how the weather, for example, affects what grows locally, or how people's lifestyles would also have influenced the type of shelter they used. For example, the nomadic Native American Plains tribes, whose lifestyle depended on following the migrating buffalo, used animal skins on tepees that could be put up and taken down quickly and transported easily. In contrast, the Algonquian Native Americans, who were farmers and lived near woodland, used stripped bark on wigwams to create a more permanent structure. And the Inuit communities of the Arctic make shelters where there are no trees and few animals, building igloos from snow.

What types of shelters do animals build? Some, such as rabbits and badgers, build underground burrows – warrens for rabbits and setts for badgers. Badgers' setts even include a toilet area! And how about the magnificent mounds up to 10m (33ft) high and 15m (50ft) wide, made by tiny termites from mud, saliva, chewed wood and faeces. Incredible!

MAKING FIRE

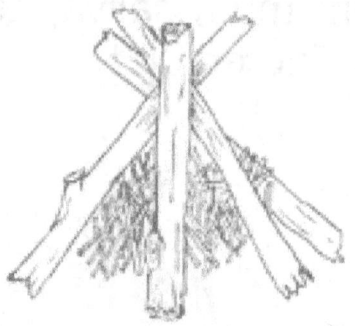

    Charles Darwin thought fire-making to be one of humankind's most significant achievements. It's easy to see why. For hundreds of thousands of years, fire has been used to light up the dark, fend off predators and keep us warm and dry. Its introduction in cooking allowed us to gain more energy from meat and plants, freeing up our time to use elsewhere. Since time immemorial it has brought us together, creating a sense of home, of belonging.

    And fire remains a potent symbol today. A fire transforms an ordinary, dark camping place into one that feels cosy, safe and special. It provides a focal point, breaking down unease and giving a reason for being in nature, with other people. We still use fire to keep away bugs and cook food. The flickering flames transfix our eyes, warm our hands and touch something ancient within us. Even a small fairy fire bursting into flame can be magical, awe-inspiring.

Creating fire without a lighter or matches is no easy feat. Striking a fire steel requires fine motor skills, and takes focus, memory, patience, problem-solving and perseverance; success in the task creates a huge sense of achievement, mastery and self-reliance. With fire come opportunities (under adult guidance) to assess risk and take responsibility, helping to develop healthy independence. Most importantly, the wonder of witnessing the creation of this element lights up everyone's faces!

LOCATION	While fairy fires can be made in any outdoor environment, camp fires are usually only allowed in designated locations. Ideally, choose one in a natural environment.
AGE GROUP	4 years + (starting with fairy fires)
LEARNING ABOUT ...	Focus ✤ memory ✤ fine motor skills ✤ patience ✤ problem solving ✤ perseverance ✤ achievement ✤ self-reliance ✤ independence ✤ assessing risks ✤ responsibility ✤ science ✤ listening skills
KIT	→ Dry sticks, twigs and logs (if a supply of fallen ones is not available) → Logs for sitting on/marking the fire boundary (optional) → Open container of water → Cotton wool → Vaseline → Fire steel

SAFETY FIRST

Whether an adult is using a fire steel alone or the children are handling it under adult supervision, follow the safety procedures on pages 104–106. Assess each child for their individual capabilities and allow them to have a go at handling the fire steel (with an adult supervising) if you feel confident that they can do so responsibly.

→ Before lighting a fire, tie back all long hair and secure any dangling jewellery and clothing.
→ An adult must supervise lit fires at all times.
→ Keep an open container of water nearby, for first aid if needed and to put out the fire.

CAMPFIRE

Get ready

Collect dry twigs of different widths, from matchstick to finger sized, as well as branches ranging from arm thickness up to larger logs. Don't choose green wood as it's hard to burn and can create lots of smoke, and avoid yew and rhododendron as they release toxic fumes when burned. Ensure you have enough wood to keep your fire fed and burning bright for the length of your stay.

A square of logs around the fire site helps to contain the fire and marks out a safe zone to be in and the fire boundary that is not to be crossed. Push any flammable material away from the fire area, and dowse this area with water in very dry weather if necessary. Always have an open container of water nearby to put out the fire. A circle of sitting logs should be at least 2m (6ft) away from the fire.

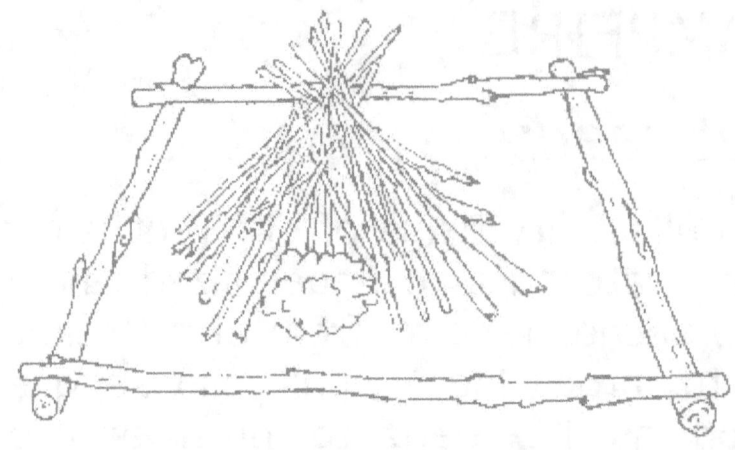

Explain the safe working zone that will be in force around everyone using a fire steel (see section entitled "Get ready"). No one should enter this zone when a fire is being started and no one should cross the fire boundary (marked either by logs or in some other way.) To ensure everyone is clear about these safety instructions, especially a large group of older children, ask them to repeat them back to you.

Get set

Demonstrate how to prepare and start a fire, before the children have a go under positive, encouraging adult supervision. First, take a ball of cotton wool and tease out the fibres; this creates an easier ignition point. Then dab a smear of Vaseline onto the fibres with your finger. This helps the fire start and the flame last longer.

Arrange the matchstick-thin twigs in a tepee shape, leaving a section open to place the cotton wool. You will also be striking the fire steel in here, so it needs to be big enough.

Go!

Hold the fire steel firmly, just above the cotton wool or to one side of it. Kneel on one knee rather than on two when striking, as this allows you to move easily away from the fire. Make sure the fire steel is the right way up (some have 'UP' marked on one side). With the blade at a 45-degree angle, strike slowly and strongly downward along the steel. Always strike away from your body and downward, and never toward someone else – be aware of which way the wind is blowing, as it can carry sparks. Striking should produce a spark that will ignite the wool, creating fire! Put away the fire-lighting kit once the fire is lit. Now let the small twigs burn, adding progressively larger pieces of wood as the fire gets going. Again, the children can help with this so long as an adult is supervising closely. An adult must watch the fire site at all times while the fire is alight.

When you are ready to leave, gently pour water onto the fire (don't chuck it), ensuring everything goes out – this is great fun! A stick can be used to mix the ash with water.

FAIRY FIRES

Fairy fires are great for younger children. They're also useful to give everyone in a large group a chance of making fire, in which case you might want to call them 'fire-starting training', or something similar, instead of 'fairy fires'!

Get ready

Demonstrate the use of the fire steel to light cotton wool, as described above.

KIT	→ Cotton wool
	→ Vaseline
	→ Clam shells (available from fishmongers), 1 per child, or baking trays, clean tin boxes or any open heatproof containers
	→ Fire steel

Get set

As with the campfire, tease out the cotton wool and smear Vaseline onto the fibres.

Our favourite choice of fireproof container is a clam shell, as it is both natural and beautiful. Putting a small dot of Vaseline onto the shell helps prevent the cotton wool blowing away.

Place the cotton wool on top of the Vaseline in the shell.

> ### TRY THIS!
> **You may want to experiment with other easily flammable materials. The tinder-dry fungus King Alfred's cake (Daldinia concentrica) is great! As ever, collect natural resources responsibly, without overharvesting.**

Go!

One by one, under close adult supervision, everyone has a go at lighting their fires! Watch the fairy fire as it flares up, burns brightly and then dies down.

Endings

Ask the children how it felt to start a fire. What was the best way of striking the fire steel? Which techniques does everyone think our ancestors may have used? Perhaps they bashed flint together to make a spark or created friction heat by drilling one stick against another.

You could talk about what fire is useful for and how it could be dangerous. (see section entitled "Endings" for some ideas about this.)

CHIMNEY KETTLE

What could be more comforting than a hot drink when you're outside on a wet, chilly day? It was probably this thought that inspired Irish fisherman Patrick Kelly, way back in the 1890s, to develop an efficient kettle fuelled by readily available natural items, such as small twigs and grass. Designed with an upward chimney draft, his kettle could rapidly boil water even in windy or rainy weather – perfect for use out fishing on Lough Conn. News of this invention quickly spread among anglers and today Kelly Kettles and similar devices are used around the world; essential kit for campers, hikers, kayakers and wilderness explorers.

With both fire and boiling water to contend with, using a chimney kettle does have some risks. As with other activities that involve hazards, encouraging the children to assess potential dangers, talk them through and think of ways in which they can be limited helps build a healthy approach to managing risk, increasing self-esteem, self-reliance and confidence. By asking the children to memorize and follow instructions, this activity encourages focus and listening skills. And preparing and sharing hot drinks when you're out in nature is a special way of bonding with others and with nature.

This is a great piece of kit, whether you're using it to sterilize water out in the wild, to make small contained fire to warm your hands on a cold day or make a delicious cup of hot chocolate.

LOCATION	Any outdoor location, but permission from the landowner may be needed in certain places, such as parks and protected woodland. Always check.
AGE GROUP	4 years +
LEARNING ABOUT ...	Managing risk ❋ responsibility ❋ self-esteem ❋ self-reliance ❋ confidence ❋ safe tool use ❋ focus ❋ memory ❋ listening skills ❋ social skills ❋ connecting with nature
KIT	→ Chimney kettle (empty or pre-filled with cold water with stopper in place) → Twigs or other natural combustible materials if a supply of dry ones is not likely to be available → Fire steel, cotton wool and vaseline → Thick gardening gloves → Cups, 1 per person → Your chosen beverage (ours is hot chocolate!) → Open container of water (to fill kettle, if needed, and as a safety precaution

SAFETY FIRST

→ Ensure the stopper is not inserted into the spout during boiling.
→ Whether an adult is using a fire steel alone or the children are handling it under adult supervision, follow the safety procedures on pages 105–6. Assess each child for their individual capabilities and allow them to have a go at handling the fire steel or pouring the kettle (with an adult supervising) if you feel confident that they can do so responsibly.
→ The lit kettle must be supervised at all times by an adult with a clear understanding of its use. Never leave a fire unattended.
→ Keep an open container of water nearby, to put out the fire if needed.

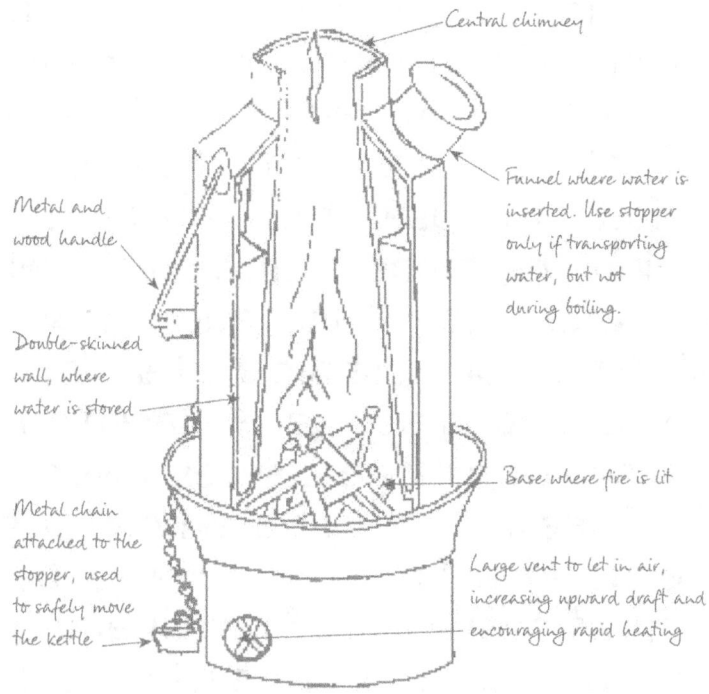

Get ready

As a safety precaution, clear potentially flammable natural materials, such as leaf litter, 1m (3ft) away from around the kettle. If necessary, in very dry conditions, dowse the area with water. Explain about the safe working zone that will be in force around everyone using a fire steel (see section entitled "Get ready"). To make the area even safer, place a square boundary of twigs at a 1m (3ft) distance around the kettle and explain that no one is to enter this area or run near it. Gather everyone round and show them the kettle with all its parts (see illustration opposite). Give a dummy demonstration on how to use the kettle safely, following the steps below. Show where the water goes in and how the small-sized combustible materials (such as twigs and grass) are placed in the fire base, with larger pieces inserted in the chimney. Demonstrate how to start a fire using a fire steel, with a ball of Vaseline-smeared cotton wool and a fire lighter, as described in section entitled "Get set".

Get set

Allow the children to take part as much as possible, asking them at each stage to tell you what they need to do next. Gather dry combustible materials, such as twigs, grass and pine cones, and prepare the cups with a drink of your choice. Fill the kettle with water, if needed, filling to just below the funnel to ensure that the water will not spit out when boiling. Do not replace the stopper as this will lead to a build-up of pressure during boiling, which risks the stopper popping out and hot water spraying around!

Place the fire base securely on level ground, with the hole facing the wind for extra draft. Dab a smear of Vaseline onto the cotton wool and place it in the fire base, then build a tepee of small twigs above it. Make sure the twigs allow room for the kettle to be placed securely on top.

Go!

Children can try to light the fire using the fire steel, following the instructions and safety advice given in section entitled "Go!", with positive, encouraging supervision from an adult. If you have a large group and it won't be possible for all to try to light the kettle, you may wish to bring fairy fire kit (see section entitled "FAIRY FIRES"). Then everyone can practise this skill, ready to take a turn with the kettle the next time!

Cross-section of base, with cotton wool.   Cross-section of base, with teepee of twigs.   Teepee of twigs built up higher in base.

Once the fire is going, the kettle handler should put on their gloves. Using both hands, grip the wire either side of the wooden part of the handle and hold the handle at a 90-degree angle to the kettle (not above the chimney as you could get burned). Lift the kettle and place it on the fire base. You will then be able to add additional fuel through the top of the chimney, to keep the fire going for as long as needed. To prevent burns, never drop in material directly above the chimney but feed it in by slightly flicking it in from the side.

We encourage using a fire steel to light the kettle as it will not run out of fuel or cease to work if wet – and it's a lot more fun than using matches! However, if you prefer to use matches and/or a lighter, then the kettle fire can also be lit through the hole with the chimney in place.

In a matter of minutes (3–5) in all weather conditions, the water will come to a rolling boil and steam will start coming through the spout. To prevent burns, use two gloved hands to lift the kettle off the fire base as described opposite. To pour, hold the wooden handle and use your other hand to hold and lift the chain to tilt the kettle. Again, a child can do this under close observation, if thought capable. Always pour into cups placed on the floor, to avoid scalding hands. Place the kettle in a safe area while the fire burns out naturally (later, you can pour water on it to ensure it's completely out, then tip the contents onto the ground).

Allow the drinks to cool a little, then enjoy them!

Endings

Taking time out with a warm drink in a natural setting creates a calm, contemplative opportunity to discuss how everyone present feels, what they have achieved with Forest School activities that day, or on a previous one, and what they may like to try again or for the first time. For example, they may want to research making different drinks, perhaps using wild foods (see section entitled "WILD FOOD").

You could also discuss where you might find different natural materials that would be good for burning in the kettle, such as bark peeled from a fallen, dead tree, dry grass in a meadow or pine cones in an evergreen forest. To empower the children with a sense of independence, ownership and responsibility for the kettle, talk through the safe working practices and why they are needed.

And, of course, you can simply sit back quietly, enjoying your drink and taking in the surroundings.

WILD FOOD

Through the seasons nature offers a wealth of food: fresh young leaves in spring, sweet flowers in summer and juicy fruits and crunchy nuts in autumn. In fact the variety of wild foods available far outstrips the relatively limited fresh foods on supermarket shelves. Foraging for food is an ancient activity; our hunter-gatherer ancestors used to do it all the time to eat.

Wild foods often taste completely different to anything you have tried before. My son loves to pick edible berries and try out new foraged foods – some go down well while others, judging by his reaction, are more of an acquired taste! Wild foods are often packed full of vitamins and minerals and have a variety of healing benefits. However, some plants can be very poisonous so only pick what you can positively identify. If in doubt, leave it alone! As with any new food, those that are edible may not agree with everyone so it's always good to sample a little bit first before handling and eating large quantities. When gathering food, avoid sources of pollution, such as roadsides, crops sprayed with herbicides and pesticides and dog-walking spots.

We share this planet with many species who rely on this natural larder as their main and only source of food. With this in mind think sustainably, spread the foraging over as large an area as possible, and never overharvest or uproot any plant. Follow local regulations about what you can and cannot pick and, if necessary, check with the landowner first.

The plants suggested here are common and easy to identify, but feel free to do your own research and expand your list of edible wild foods. Foraging is such a wonderful experience for everyone and truly connects us to our surroundings. You will never look at 'weeds' in the same way again!

This healthy, active pastime deepens a child's connection with nature. It encourages thinking about where food comes from and about how to use resources sustainably. It can inspire a desire to cook and find out about nutrition. Learning to identify different natural species leads on to making connections and communication, to curiosity and focus, and to feelings of self-esteem and confidence. Finding delicious natural food and knowing its benefits can foster a sense of independence.

LOCATION	Variety of locations, including woodland, parks, wasteland, gardens, grass, hedgerows and along waterways
AGE GROUP	4 years +
LEARNING ABOUT ...	Connecting with nature ⊛ species identification ⊛ being active ⊛ curiosity ⊛ focus ⊛ self-esteem ⊛ confidence ⊛ independence ⊛ communication ⊛ sustainability ⊛ nutrition

SAFETY FIRST
Positive identification of edible wild foods is vital as many plants are poisonous. Take a field guide or use your phone to access a website with pictures of edible plants, and choose wild foods that can be easily identified, such as those featured here.

When you begin to forage for tasty natural morsels, rummaging around shrubs, picking through leaf litter, linking knowledge of the seasons and location to find just what you were hoping to find, you will begin to see the world differently: the hunter-gatherer within you will awaken!

CLEAVERS JUICE DRINK

KIT	INGREDIENTS
→ Clean gardening gloves for each forager	→ 1 cupful foraged cleavers per cup of juice
→ Water for washing the cleavers and hands (plus soap for hands)	→ Apple juice
→ 2 cups per forager	
→ Pestle or something similar (if not making a pounding stick)	
→ Potato peeler (for older children, if making a pounding stick)	

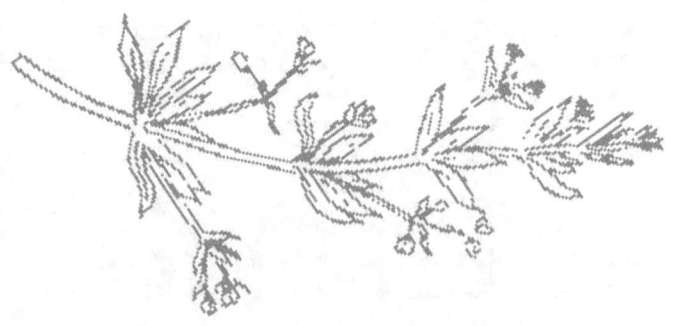

Cleavers *(Galium aparine)* is known by many other names, including 'goosegrass' (because geese love eating it) and 'sticky willy' (because it will stick to most things!). Many children will already know this creeping plant and have probably had lots of fun chucking it at their friends and seeing how it clings to their clothes (especially funny when it hangs around unnoticed on their backs!).

The square-shaped stem, leaves and fruit of this annual plant all bear tiny hooks that cling on and aid the plant's dispersal. The leaves are narrow and lance-shaped and usually grow in whorls of six to eight around the stem, which can grow up to 3m (10ft) along the ground and up and over other plants. Tiny four-petalled white flowers can appear between May to August, turning into round fruit.

Cleavers is common in moist grassy places, hedgerows, woods, shingle, gardens, wasteland and field edges. In traditional herbal medicine, this plant was said to have a cleansing effect when applied externally, to help the healing of cuts and wounds and to alleviate many kinds of skin problems. Forage in spring and summer, before the plant seeds and becomes slightly woody.

Get ready

Collect a small sample of the plant before the activity begins and show this to all foragers. Give each forager gloves as the plant can be scratchy. Cleavers can also occasionally cause an irritable reaction if it comes into contact with skin, so wear gloves as a precaution (the juice is perfectly safe to drink).

Get set

You can make your own pounding stick to use instead of a pestle. Find a blunt-ended stick about two finger-widths across and peel off the bark using a potato peeler (see section entitled "Get ready" for instructions about the safe working zone and the use of potato peelers).

Head off foraging and gather up those cleavers! For one cup of juice you will need a cup full of cleavers (young tips only) plus one spare handful (any part of the plant) to strain the cleaver juice.

Go!

Wash your hands and the cleavers. Place them in a cup with a splash of apple juice.

Pound the cleavers with the pestle (no need to wear a glove for this), until all the green juice comes out the leaves. Add more apple juice if the drink needs topping up.

There will naturally be bits and pieces in the mix. To strain these, mat together a small handful of cleavers over the other drinking cup and strain the juice through it.

Your cleavers juice drink is ready to try. Enjoy!

ELDERFLOWER FRITTERS

ELDERFLOWER FRITTERS

KIT
- Container for collected elderflowers
- Dish towel
- Mixing bowl
- Whisk/fork
- Deep frying pan (or deep-fat fryer)
- Kitchen paper

INGREDIENTS
- 1 elderflower head per fritter
- Sunflower oil, for frying
- Sugar, for sprinkling

FOR THE BATTER (SERVES 4)
- 1 egg
- 100g/3½oz/¾ cup flour
- 140ml/¼ pint water at room temperature
- Pinch salt

Elder *(Sambucus nigra)* is a small tree or deciduous shrub that can be found in woods, parks, hedgerows, scrub and wasteland. The leaves are pinnate with five serrated leaflets. Large clusters of small, creamy white flowers appear in late spring, turning into small, glossy black berries in autumn. The flowers have a distinctive sweet smell that strongly resembles their taste.

This is a traditional medicinal plant with many uses; consuming its juice and fruit is popular as a remedy for colds and flu, for example. It was also reputed to soften the skin and a bottle of elder water was a common feature of Victorian households, to help remove freckles and sunburn. Many legends and magical beliefs are linked to elder: planting it at your back door was believed to ward off witches! The plant is versatile and can be used in a variety of recipes, such as sorbets, cordials, jellies, ice cream and jam. These fritters can be cooked on the coals of a campfire or at home.

Get ready

Before you start, show the foragers a flowerhead so they know what they're looking for. Give each forager a container to collect them in.

Get set

Look for flowers that are free from insects, as well as open and fresh – they should not fall off when the stem is gently shaken. Leave about 2.5cm (1in) of stalk attached to the flowerheads as you pick them. Allow one flowerhead per fritter (if very large they can make more). Put them in a container to keep them intact and fresh.

Go!

When you have returned to the cooking area, wash your hands and carefully wash the flowerheads in cold water. Shake off excess water and place on a dish towel. Mix the egg, flour, water and salt to create a batter with the consistency of double/heavy cream. Holding the stalks, dip the flowerheads into the batter, coating them fully.

Heat about 5cm (2in) of oil in the pan. When the oil is hot, turn down the heat slightly and deep-fry the batter-coated flowerheads in small batches until the batter turns golden brown. Place them on a kitchen towel to soak up excess oil and trim off the stalk. Sprinkle sugar over them and serve warm. Your wildflower treat is ready!

BLACKBERRY ICE

BLACKBERRY ICE

KIT	INGREDIENTS
→ Clean gardening gloves for each forager	→ 450g/1lb/3½ cups fresh blackberries
→ Water for washing the blackberries (and soap for washing hands)	→ 140ml/¼ pint of water
	→ 100g/3½oz/½ cup caster sugar
→ Container to collect blackberries	→ 1 egg white
→ Pan	
→ Sieve/mouli	
→ Bowl	
→ Whisk	
→ Freezer-proof dish	
→ Plastic wrap	

Blackberry *(Rubus genus)* bushes can be found in woods, hedges, scrub, gardens, wasteland and parks. There are many hybrids and varieties that yield slightly different-tasting fruits and finding your favourite can be part of your exploration.

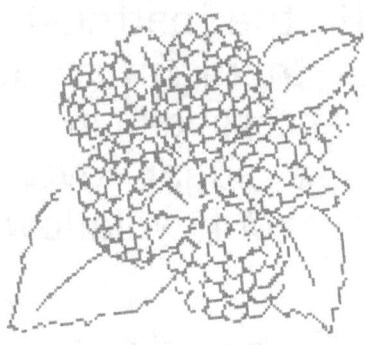

The blackberry is a deciduous, woody shrub that is covered in sharp prickles strong enough to tear through clothing. The five-petal, white or pink flowers appear around May to September, turning to ripe, glossy black fruits from August to November. As a loose rule, the sweetest-tasting fruit are those that appear first in August.

Many insects, birds and mammals eat blackberries, and blackberry pips found in the stomach of a Neolithic man discovered on the Essex coast indicate our own species appears to have enjoyed eating them as far back as prehistoric times. (Perhaps our long history of foraging this wild fruit is why it is the one best known by us today.) Blackberries are a particularly healthy and nutritious fruit, containing vitamin C along with other vitamins and minerals; the seeds are rich in omega 3 and 6 oils, as well as protein and fibre.

Get ready

Hike out to your chosen spot. Remember blackberry bushes guard themselves well with tough prickles, so wear suitable clothing and gloves when picking fruit.

Get set

Of course it goes without saying that some of these juicy blackberries will need to be eaten on site (clean berries and hands for this), but try to keep around 450g (1lb) for your recipe so you can taste the fruit in a different way. Place the blackberries in your container and take them home.

Go!

Wash the blackberries and set to one side. Boil the water and sugar together until all the sugar melts, to make a syrup. While it cools, pass the blackberries through a sieve or mouli. Once the syrup is cool, mix in the strained juice.

Beat the egg white with a whisk in a bowl until it forms soft peaks. Fold in the blackberry syrup. Put into your freezer-proof dish, cover with plastic wrap and place in the freezer. When it has become mushy with ice crystals (check at 30 minutes), take out of the freezer and stir to break down into smaller crystals. Allow to freeze again for 30 minutes, then take out and stir again. Repeat a third time. Put back in the freezer and leave until it has set (about three hours). Scoop out and serve your yummy blackberry ice. Share with friends your foraging journey as well as the ice!

Endings

Did the foragers like their wild food and was it fun to share this experience with the people around them? If yes, why? Would they like to try more wild food? If they would, there's a wonderful outdoor larder waiting for them to discover! Can anyone invent some wild-food recipes? Remind everyone only to eat wild food that has been identified by someone who knows what they are looking for, as some plants are toxic, while others are rare and precious.

It's interesting to talk about where our food comes from. All supermarket fresh food had a wild ancestor that we have cultivated. For example, sweetcorn has a dark-coloured, hard-husked relative called teosinte. You can also talk about nutrition – what our bodies need to grow and for energy – and the healing aspects of plants.

Do the children think any animals would eat the food they tried? Canada geese will munch on cleavers, many bird species feast on elderberries in autumn, and the comma butterfly loves to feed on blackberry flowers. Talk about the sustainable use of resources: never overharvesting, but leaving plants for other species to use, and roots and seeds for future crops.

Wildlife Team Games

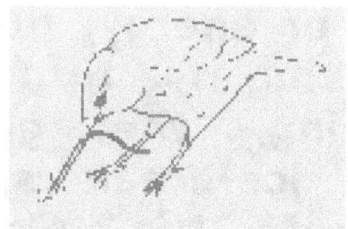

Interacting as a group can be a complicated business for us all, especially if the relationships are new to us. We all have our strengths and 'lesser strengths' within this context. We may find that we pigeonhole ourselves or that the group assigns us to a certain role that we would not necessarily have chosen. These interactions are no less complicated for children. Some children are not afraid to speak up and are happy to take a central role, but others may be shy. Some may find it hard to occupy what might appears to be an insignificant role, while others may not want to take part at all for fear of 'losing' or being embarrassed.

Wildlife team games provide an opportunity for each child to explore these interactions and develop social skills. Full of energy, purpose and joy, and giving rise to a real sense of wellbeing, the games are fantastic ice-breakers, taking attention off the players and focusing it onto the activity. They allow players to occupy a range of roles, as different animals for example, and give everyone an equally valued voice. These games show how all things in nature, including ourselves, are connected, helping to build relationships, confidence and a sense of belonging. They are a fantastic way to start the day and allow us all to feel part of the team!

WHAT'S MY ANIMAL?

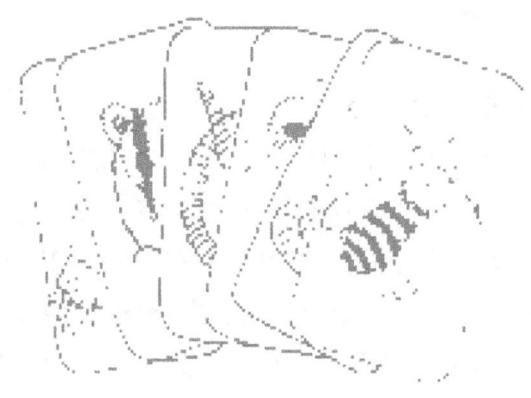

This game does not involve any running around but is still very lively! It's hard not to giggle and fall about in anticipation as each question gets closer to the discovery of the animal ... or not, as the case may be! All depends on the skills of the detective.

A guessing game is a playful way to learn new facts about animals. The use of questions and answers develops language, and the unravelling of the mystery requires logical thinking, deduction and the making of connections. We've found this to be a great activity to pull a group together, because it provides an interesting point of focus, a satisfying challenge and an opportunity for teamwork.

Get ready

Create some animal cards. Choosing animals that live locally can help to reinforce the children's bond with their environment but nothing is set in stone – what sort of animals would the children like in the game? The cards should show the animal's name and picture, perhaps downloaded from the Internet, cut out from a magazine, photocopied from a book or even drawn yourself (if you're feeling creative!).

Back the paper with sturdy cardboard. Line the top edge of each animal card with masking tape (above the picture to ensure it's pinned the correct way up) and stick a safety pin through the tape.

If gaps in knowledge may hinder the game, it may help to talk through the animal facts linked to each chosen animal before the game begins. Try making an animal fact sheet (see section entitled "ANIMAL FACT SHEET").

Get set

Choose who will be the detective first (everyone will eventually get a turn). One of the other children picks an animal card, without showing it to the detective, and pins it to the detective's back.

LOCATION	Anywhere but preferably outside in an area where at least some of the featured animals live
AGE GROUP	5 years +
NUMBER OF PLAYERS	2 + (the more the merrier!)
LEARNING ABOUT...	Logical and deductive thinking ⊕ language ⊕ teamwork ⊕ focus ⊕ animal ecology
KIT	→ Animal picture cards → Animal fact sheet (optional) → Masking tape → Safety pins

ANIMAL FACT SHEET

COMMON MOLE — Mammal ⊕ Velvety dark grey fur ⊕ Long pointed nose ⊕ Four feet (shovel-like, five-clawed front feet) ⊕ Tiny eyes ⊕ Eats earthworms, slugs and insect larvae ⊕ Lives in underground tunnels, mostly in pastures, gardens and woodland ⊕ Cannot fly ⊕ Does not hibernate ⊕ Active day and night ⊕ Does not lay eggs ⊕ Lives alone

BADGER — Mammal ⊕ Black-and-white fur ⊕ Four feet and strong claws ⊕ Small eyes ⊕ Eats mostly earthworms and insects but can eat meat, fruits, cereals ⊕ Lives mostly in underground tunnels called 'setts', preferably near woodland, fields and meadows ⊕ Cannot fly ⊕ Does not hibernate ⊕ Nocturnal ⊕ Does not lay eggs ⊕ Lives socially

COMMON EARTHWORM — Invertebrate ⊕ No fur but has bristles on segmented body ⊕ No feet ⊕ No eyes ⊕ Eats soil and organic matter ⊕ Lives in underground soil burrows ⊕ Cannot fly ⊕ Does not hibernate ⊕ Nocturnal ⊕ Lays eggs ⊕ Lives alone

HONEY BEE — Insect ⊕ Hair on body ⊕ Six legs ⊕ Five eyes ⊕ Eats pollen and nectar ⊕ Builds wax nests in hollow trees ⊕ Can fly ⊕ Hibernates ⊕ Diurnal (active in the day) ⊕ Lays eggs ⊕ Lives socially

The detective turns their back on the group to show the animal card, then turns to face the group to begin the questioning!

TRY THIS!

> **Older children who know lots of animal facts can do without prompt cards, meaning they can keep playing for as long as they want. Very useful on a rainy day or during long car journeys!**

Go!

The detective now asks questions to discover what animal they have become, such as: 'Can I fly?', 'Do I live underground?', 'Do I have fur?' The group can **TRY THIS!** only give yes or no answers. When the detective feels they have the right answer, they can guess who they are. Once they have discovered their identity, it's another detective's turn.

Endings

Encourage discussion about the animals on the cards. For example, if you have a honey bee, you might talk about how they help plants create new fruits and vegetables through pollination. Honey bees fly from flower to flower looking for both nectar (a sugary liquid made by flowers) to make into honey, and pollen (the plant's powdery male genes) to eat. As they do so, they also transfer the male pollen to the female parts of the flower, helping to create new seeds. Bees can see colours in the ultra-violet range, which we humans cannot see, and to them some markings on flowers look like airplane landing strips, guiding them to brush past the pollen on their way to the nectar! A mutually beneficial relationship.

Which is each child's favourite animal (or animals) and why? Did they prefer to be the detective or a team player? Why?

FOREST FIRE

Imagine fire sweeping through a forest, crackling and hissing, the clouds of smoke, the burning heat, the orange and red flames leaping from branch to branch. This game is full of the energy of fire! It's an exciting way to start the day, before attempting some more focused activities, when everyone's full of beans and the need to move prevails.

This activity is also a great way to bring a group together through teamwork and strategic thinking, especially when the fire grows and players must move as one to get more fuel. Trying to avoid the flames builds confidence and self-reliance, and all that turning and ducking improves physical skills and co-ordination. But most of all this game is uplifting and just plain hilarious. Players dash about, the forest fire forgets who's attached to whom and darts off in different directions, and tension mounts as the fire chooses who to chase next!

We absolutely love this game, as have all the children we've ever played it with!

Get ready

As the children are likely to veer off in all directions, set the boundaries of a roughly rectangular space in which the game will be played, making sure the area is big enough so that everyone can run around within it. The players will run between two safe places at either end of the rectangle. Choose who will be the fire – the game often starts with an adult playing the first flickering flame.

Get set

Ask the children to think about what animals might live in the area. Together, come up with a list of three or four species likely to be found in the place you're playing: for example, if you are in a woodland you might choose an owl, a fox, a rabbit or butterfly.

Everyone who's not the fire can choose to be one of these species, creating groups among the players.

LOCATION	A clearing in woodland, home to a variety of animal life in a setting where the children can imagine a forest fire, is best for atmosphere. However, any outdoor space where children can run is fine.
AGE GROUP	4 years +
NUMBER OF PLAYERS	6 +
LEARNING ABOUT ...	Being active ⊕ physical skills ⊕ teamwork ⊕ self-reliance ⊕ confidence ⊕ strategic thinking ⊕ role play
KIT	None needed

Now everyone takes up their positions! One of the safe places is the starting point for all the players. The fire stands somewhere between this starting point and the other safe place.

Go!

The fire calls out one of the animals (for example, 'OWL!'). All those animals have to make a run for it past the fire to the safe place on the other side. Just as real fire spreads, anyone caught by the fire will then also become fire; these players will now hold hands. Now all the fire players need to work together to decide who to call for next, and remember to move as one to catch them.

If some players make it to the safe place without being caught, they must now run back to the safe place on the opposite side.

Again, fire calls out – perhaps this time for 'FOX!'. Now all the foxes have to dash and dodge for the other side. If the fire players decide to shout out 'FOREST FIRE!' everyone has to run to the other side. As players are caught they join hands and the fire grows. The game carries on in this way running between sides until one person is left – this is the winner!

TRY THIS!

Anyone who runs outside the boundaries automatically becomes fire, so take care!

Now the game can start again. The winner can choose to be the fire or select someone else for that role. If everyone wants to, they can keep playing until they've all had a go at the different roles.

Endings

You could have a discussion about forest fires. What might happen if people were careless with fire in a woodland? How can we avoid that? What natural events, such as lightning, may trigger fires?

Fires are sometimes used deliberately to help sustain some landscapes. For example, on upland heathlands in the UK rotational burning helps to maintain a mosaic of habitats that support an incredible variety of associated plant and animal life. A similar method is used in Canadian forests. We use fire for cooking and keeping ourselves warm, to name only two examples – in fact fire changed the course of human existence (see section entitled "MAKING FIRE"). It is a powerful force that must be treated with respect.

If the children are inspired to make their own fire, see section entitled "MAKING FIRE" for some exciting fire activities. Using a chimney kettle (see section entitled "CHIMNEY KETTLE") is another good way of interacting with fire.

PREDATORS TRACK PREY

This game introduces the relationship between predators and prey, with one team playing the role of tracking predators and the other the elusive prey. It is full of the thrills of hunting and hiding, and the anticipation of which team will succeed. We've played this game with different age groups and found it usually begins with lots of running around and loud, joyful talking, but then, as if by magic, the teams are taken over by their roles. The prey assume a silent, purposeful stillness as they hide from the approaching predator; at the same time the predators come together as a team, determined to catch their prey.

This very active game needs focus and strategic thinking as both teams work out how best to survive. The woodland really comes alive for the children as they explore it with all their senses and understand it for the first time through the eyes of predators and prey. It develops teamwork and communication as the players need to rely on each other to win. And, best of all, whether the children are predators or prey, it's a fantastic, fun-filled game that offers many animal tactics to try, and you can't help but get caught up in all the excitement.

LOCATION	Woodland big enough to hide in, with plenty of trees and bushes to provide cover
AGE GROUP	4 years +
NUMBER OF PLAYERS	6 + (including 2 adults, 1 per team)
LEARNING ABOUT ...	Strategic thinking ❀ focus ❀ using the senses ❀ teamwork ❀ communication ❀ being active ❀ predator–prey relationships ❀ connection with nature ❀ role play
KIT	None needed. Use the natural materials in the area (if sticks are likely to be in short supply you could bring some with you).

Get ready

Gather everyone round and explain that a predator is an animal that hunts and eats other animals. The prey is the animal that is eaten. For example, a fox will catch and eat a rabbit, so the fox is the predator and the rabbit is the prey. The prey is always trying to survive but so is the predator. It's all about survival.

In this game there will be two teams, one the predators and one the prey (everyone can swap roles at the end to get a turn at being both). The prey will find a place in the woodland to hide from the predators, who will come in search of them. Just as in nature, when predators look, smell and listen out for signs of their prey, the prey in this game will also leave signs. These will be stick arrows on the ground showing which way the prey have gone.

As a group, gather as many sticks as possible for the prey to use as tracking arrows. If you haven't brought sticks and there are not many on the ground, you can collect other natural objects like stones or pine cones, or decide to draw arrows in the soil.

Get set

Decide as a group who will be in the two teams: predators and prey. There needs to be at least one adult per team to be with the children as they roam through the woodland. Remind everyone they will get a chance to be both.

Before the prey set out, it can be helpful for them to talk together (out of the predators' earshot!) about the direction they will be going and where they would like to hide.

The prey have 15 minutes to place the tracking arrows and hide all together.

> **TRY THIS!**
>
> **If boredom or impatience is likely to set in while the predators wait, try a game of What's My Animal? (see section entitled "WHAT'S MY ANIMAL?").**

Go!

Synchronize watches.

Now the prey head off! Although the arrows must be easy to see, they should not lead all the way to the prey but instead stop about 15m (50ft) away from the prey's hiding place. Mark this final spot with a cross (X) made of sticks.

After 15 minutes is up, predators go track your prey! The predators now follow the arrows to try to find the prey. When the arrows stop and they find the X, the predators begin to search the area as a group (without splitting up), to find their food.

If the prey are found, the predators have won. If the prey can avoid being seen, and jump out together on the predators as they pass by, shouting 'STOP!', then the prey have survived and won the game.

Predators can now become prey and prey on the predators!

Endings

There are lots of interesting ways in which you can talk about predator–prey relationships in nature. Can the children think of any special features that prey animals have developed in order to survive? Speed to escape capture can be seen in hares, for example, who have powerful legs that allow them to run fast to escape from hunting foxes. The stick insect uses camouflage to blend in and hide. The bee has its stripes that warn, 'Beware, if you eat me you will be stung!' And tortoises have a hard shell that acts as protective armour.

And what about the predators – what might help them catch their food? Hunting as a team allows wolves to catch bigger prey, like bison, that would be impossible to manage alone. Speed and sharp teeth for catching and consuming prey are found in cheetahs and mako sharks. Think too that herbivores (plant eaters), such as hares, could be seen in some ways as 'predators' of plants. To survive, some plants (such as ragwort) have become poisonous if eaten, while others (such as brambles) have developed thorns. Which survival tactics do the children think most helped them when being predators or prey?

These complex predator–prey relationships have in some cases evolved over hundreds of thousands of years and have come to offer some benefits for all life. For example, predators help to keep prey numbers down to a level that the environment can support. The number of predators around will depend on the numbers of prey needed to feed them. Predators can easily catch sick animals and eat them, which helps prevent disease spreading through the prey animals. In this way populations of both predators and prey are kept healthy and balanced.

WEB OF LIFE

Everything is connected – air, water, soil, plants and animals. All the elements of life are bound together in an amazing balanced system that has evolved to allow for survival on this planet. This is the great web of life. Whatever happens to one of its strands has an effect on the system as a whole.

In this game, creating a network of connections makes the concept of an ecosystem real for the children. It can develop a sense of community and of belonging, as well as an awareness of the importance of each individual player and of the particular strand within the web of life that they are representing. This activity shows how what happens to one part of the network affects all the other parts, opens children up to ideas about experimentation, cause and effect, evolution, empathy, conservation and sustainability. Discussing these concepts and outcomes develops language, focus and curiosity.

LOCATION	This game can be played anywhere but a natural space offering a diverse range of plants, birds and animals that can be seen and heard is ideal.
AGE GROUP	5 years +
NUMBER OF PLAYERS	5 +
LEARNING ABOUT ...	Ecology ❀ teamwork ❀ belonging ❀ curiosity ❀ focus ❀ nature connections ❀ empathy ❀ sustainability ❀ language skills
KIT	Ball of wool or string

It's always amazing to see the deeper thinking and the wonder and awe that this game can trigger.

Get ready

Set the scene. Explain that an ecosystem is comprised of all living things in an area (animals, plants, fish, fungi, bacteria, etc) and how they interact with each other and the nonliving things of this environment (soil, the sun's energy, weather, rocks, air, etc). All these elements have their role to play in helping to keep the whole habitat going in a balanced way. We can visualize this as a web, with strands connecting everything in the ecosystem. In this game we are going to build our own web of life.

Get set

Choose the leader, either an adult or an older child with some knowledge of ecology. This leader is going to ask questions about connections between animals, plants, soil, water and air and get everyone thinking about how these come together to form an ecosystem. Everyone sits in a circle around the leader, who stands in the middle with the ball of string or wool.

Go!

Go!

The leader starts by asking someone to name a plant that grows in the area around you. The first to answer is given the end of the string. This child now represents that plant.

The leader then asks who can name an animal that may live in or eat this plant. The player who answers is given the line of string to hold, which is still attached to the first 'plant'. This second player is now that animal connected to the plant through its need of it!

Next, the leader asks the group who might eat this animal. When someone shouts out a possible predator, they are given the string line and now represent that animal.

This sequence of connections continues as the leader keeps asking questions to bring in new animals and plants, as well as other elements, such as water, soil and air. For example:
- Where might this animal drink?
- What plants might be found in this water?

- Which insect might live on this plant?

Continue until every child in the group is holding the string and the web is formed. This now represents an ecosystem.

Now, to show the importance of each aspect of the web and how loss, change or damage to any one of them can affect the whole community, a player is taken from the web, with a real-life cause given for this. For example, if one child is a tree, say that they have been cut down by a logger. The tree dies and the child representing it tugs on the string. Anyone who can feel this tugging has been affected by the loss of the tree; they in turn begin to pull on the string, affecting yet more players. This continues until everyone feels the impact of the death of the tree. In this way everyone will realize that we are all connected and that the whole web will be affected by harm or disruption to any one part.

Endings

Even the smallest of things that we may overlook or call weeds or pests have their valued place within an ecosystem. For example, common nettles, which we humans consider a weed, are the primary food source of the larvae of the breathtaking peacock butterfly, whose appearance in spring brings joy after the dark winter months. Peacock butterflies in turn help to pollinate many species of plants and will themselves be food for birds such as great tits. A similar tale can be told about milkweed and monarch butterflies. Pollination helps not only the plants but humans too, by creating food crops we eat such as papaya, pumpkins and apples (see section entitled "Endings").

Talk about what can be done to help sustain an ecosystem, such as limiting logging in the rainforest, where each tree can sustain hundreds of species. The trees of a rainforest also clean our air (by taking in carbon dioxide and releasing oxygen), and prevent soil erosion. You could discuss extinction and how the loss of a species can have negative knock-on effects on the whole environment. For example, if a top predator such as the Australian dingo were to be lost, herbivores such as the kangaroo would no longer be predated and their numbers would soar. This could lead to overgrazing, leading to loss of plants, leading to loss of other herbivore species – an all-round loss.

Our planet with all its wonderful biodiversity (including us humans) is unique within our solar system – all the more reason to look after what we have.

BAT AND MOTH

This game provides a window straight onto another world – a world of sound, of darkness, of the hunter and the hunted, of amazing adaptations that animals make to survive.

Bat and Moth brings out intense focus and real joy in children, whether they are playing a bat swooping down on its prey, or a moth craftily eluding capture, or one of the trees, wiggling with excitement on the spot. The children connect with each other, transcend shyness and become fully present. Afterwards they are always full of questions about these clever creatures!

A key skill in Bat and Moth is listening, vital in absorbing verbal information as well as in building friendships. The game's different roles also provide opportunities to be active, to fine-tune the senses, to learn self-control and focus, to trust others and work with them, and to be self-reliant. The bat must listen carefully for the moth's reply, blocking out all distractions. Bats must also trust the boundary created by the trees and their own blind movements. It's only by drawing on this focus and self-sufficiency that they will succeed in capturing their prey.

Moths have to listen carefully for the bat's call and stay alert to its approaching movements. They must be stealthy, staying silent while actively avoiding capture. Trees on the other hand have to be self-controlled and work as a team to form a boundary, staying alert to the action but keeping still and only speaking if they're actually touched by a bat or moth. All in all, a truly wonderful experience!

Get ready

Tell the children all about the amazing natural phenomenon known as echolocation. Bats are supposed to be blind, but actually they can see almost as well as we can. To spot food such as moths and other insects at night, they need to use their ears rather than their eyes. Bats build up a picture of the world around them by making calls as they fly about and listening for the returning echo. This is called echolocation. By making these calls, bats can tell how far away something is, how big it is, its shape and where it's going.

LOCATION	A woodland clearing is ideal, as woods are the habitat of many bat and moth species. However, this game can be played in any open space.
AGE GROUP	4 years +
NUMBER OF PLAYERS	6 + For very big groups: → Try increasing the number of moths to 3–5. → If it's proving difficult to capture moths, the trees can take a step closer to tighten the circle.
LEARNING ABOUT ...	Being active ❂ using the senses, especially hearing ❂ focus ❂ self-reliance/control ❂ natural selection/species adaptation
KIT	A cotton scarf or other blindfold

Get set

Choose one player to be the bat and another to be the moth. Everyone else is the trees. (Everyone can take a turn at being either bat or moth.) All the trees hold hands and spread out to make a circle around the bat and moth. Tie a scarf around the bat's eyes as a blindfold. Now the bat is going to try to catch the moth!

Go!

The bat claps hands and the moth claps back. Clapping hands is the bat sending out a sound wave. The moth clapping in return is the sound bouncing back to the bat. That's echolocation! The bat now knows where the moth is and is ready to catch and eat its prey. The moth must avoid capture to survive. If the bat grabs one of the tree as it tries to track down the moth, the tree calls out 'TREE!', and the hunt continues. When the bat catches a moth, the moth can consider itself eaten! The bat carries on hunting until all the moths have been caught.

> **TRY THIS!**
>
> **Clapping several times in quick succession may make tracking down moths easier.**

Endings

Encourage the children to talk about bats and moths. Which traits, such as moving fast, listening well and being confident, are best for catching moths? And which skills, such as moving quietly, staying low to the ground and being quick, helped the moths to survive?

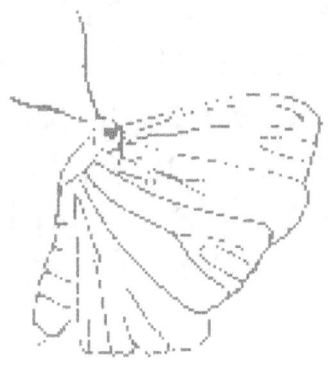

In nature, the traits that help each animal species survive are passed on from parent to baby in a process called natural selection. A fantastic example of this is the night-flying peppered moth *(Biston betularia)*, found across the world. In Britain until the 19th century these had usually been pale in colour, which helped them stay camouflaged against the light-coloured birch trees which they rested on. Any peppered moths that mutated into a darker colour were more easily seen and eaten by birds. But during the Industrial Revolution, smoke and other pollution from factories blackened the trees. Then the pale moths were no longer well camouflaged and began to be eaten in greater numbers, leaving any darker peppered moths to take over. And there's a twist to the tale. Now we are taking more care of the environment, and our trees are no longer so polluted, the pale peppered moths have returned. The way animals adapt to their environment is one of the wonders of nature!

HUNGRY BIRDS

It's spring. Imagine being a baby bird growing in your egg, inside your cosy nest. Your parents take turns keeping you safe and warm until you grow too big for your egg and crack it open using a special egg-tooth. When you come out into the world as a hatchling, your eyes are closed and you have no feathers. Your parents keep you warm and feed you – it might be fruits or it might be bugs! After a few days, you open your eyes and some downy feathers begin to grow. You explore your nest and look at the world outside. You are now a nestling. After a couple of weeks your feathers have grown, your muscles are stronger and you leave your nest for the first time. You are a fledgling, hopping on the ground while your parents teach you what to eat. Days pass. You stretch your wings and flex your muscles and you fly! As an adult bird, you look for a tasty morsel to eat, perhaps a juicy, fat worm...

> ### TRY THIS!
> **Encourage the children to imagine being a baby bird in its shell, breaking out into the world and growing up, learning all the skills it needs to survive.**

Taking on the challenges faced by birds as they search for their food can really help children connect with these amazing creatures, and they will be intrigued by the survival strategies represented by the worms too. This game really gets the children moving, as they run around all over the place in search of worms. It also encourages observation and teamwork, as well as counting and fine motor skills. This is a game full of energy and fun, which opens up a hunting bird's-eye view of the world.

LOCATION	Woodland with its varied habitats and bird species are ideal, but you can use any spacious outdoor area, such as parks and gardens, with a range of possible hiding places for the worms.
AGE GROUP	4 years +
NUMBER OF PLAYERS	2 +
LEARNING ABOUT ...	Being active ✿ observation ✿ teamwork ✿ fine motor skills ✿ counting skills ✿ role play ✿ connection with nature ✿ species survival strategies
KIT	→ 12cm (5in) lengths of wool in different colours, including bright colours – reds, yellows, blues as well as browns and greens → Double-sided sticky tape (for younger children, optional)

Get ready

Before the game starts, hide the worms (strands of differently coloured wool) around your area, remembering where you placed them. Make sure a few will be easy to find by placing some bright ones close to the starting point.

Collect two sticks for each team (four in total). Tie a strand of each colour you have hidden onto two of the four sticks. These two sticks will be used as a guide by each team to help them locate the worm colours that have been hidden. Divide the children into two teams of hungry birds, and tell them that they're going to be looking for worms to eat. Show them the outer boundary of the area where they are hunting. Beyond this boundary they won't find any worms.

Get set

Give each team a guide stick that displays all the colours they are looking for, as well as another stick that they will use for tying on all the worms they find. (If you think anyone will find tying wool onto the string too difficult, you can put double-sided sticky tape on the sticks for attaching the wool.)

Tell the children that they are young birds and must stick together, to help each other hunt for food. Set a time limit according to the age and size of your group and area: 15–20 minutes is a good starting point (for younger and smaller groups allow the longer time). To limit disappointment and a sense of losing, especially for younger players, explain that as long as they find three worms they will not be hungry – but the more worms, the merrier!

Ask the children to point out the boundary, so you are sure that they know where not to go.

Go!

Set the clock. The birds head off to find their worms! For older children the game can be made more interesting by setting a target. For example, red and blue worms are toxic and cannot be eaten, and all brown and green worms (better camouflaged and harder to spot) must be found! Reducing time allowed also increases the challenge. Teams can of course compete here, too.

When time's up, call all birds back to count up their worms!

Endings

Ask which colours of worms were easier to spot – the green or brown ones or the red ones? Was it those that were out in the open, high up, low down or tucked into a bush?

Birds also eat a wide range of insects. How can insects avoid capture? Survival strategies include being camouflaged, tasting disgusting, being poisonous, having a hard shell or a painful sting. With this in mind, how important is having a parent bird to teach the young what they can and cannot eat? What do the children think of birds now?

ANT TRAIL

Winged princess

Have you ever been mesmerized by a mass of ants moving apparently at random over the ground? And then begun to see the patterns in their movements, the way foraging worker ants create trails for others to follow to bring food and building materials back to the colony? These highly organized nests can have millions of inhabitants, all working together for the survival of the colony in a complex social structure that has inspired comparisons with human society.

This game invites children to marvel at the truly incredible achievements of ants. There are over 12,000 species of ant known (the count is rising), and they live in a wide range of habitats all over the world. They can be omnivores, herbivores, predators and scavengers, and are among our planet's most successful species.

This walking activity really pulls a group together, developing concentration, teamwork and social skills. Encouraging children to see themselves as a different species is wonderful role play, developing curiosity and the imagination and deepening their bond with the natural world.

Get ready

Plan the route for the walk. Also, to help with the role play, tell the children a little about the amazing world of ants. Large colonies (a family of ants) tend to have ants with different roles to ensure the colony survives. There are queens (sometimes one or more), who are larger than the others and lay the eggs that produce all the ants of the colony. Winged princesses become future queens once they've mated with a drone and laid eggs to found a new colony; at this point they clip their own wings and become flightless. Drones, winged like the princesses, are the only males. They die after mating with a princess, the future queen. Worker ants are the ones we normally see as they forage for food and nest materials; they are females that take care of the nest, the young and the queen. Soldier ants found in some nests (like leaf cutters) are also female workers who with their large biting heads protect the colony from invaders and predators. They can also cut through and carry objects that smaller worker ants cannot manage.

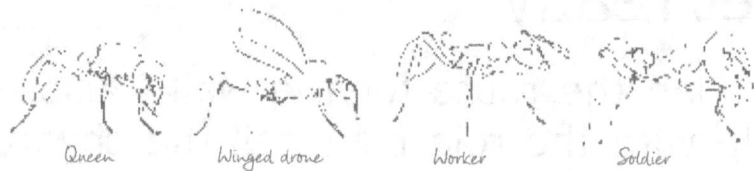

Queen   Winged drone   Worker   Soldier

LOCATION	Any natural place that's suitable for walking
AGE GROUP	4 years +
NUMBER OF PLAYERS	4 +
LEARNING ABOUT ...	Being active ⊛ concentration ⊛ teamwork ⊛ society (ours and other species') ⊛ communication ⊛ role play ⊛ curiosity ⊛ imagination ⊛ connection with nature
KIT	None needed

Ants can carry loads 50–100 times their own body weight and even heavier objects when working as a group. They communicate with each other through vibrations and scent (using chemicals called pheromones, for example), marking out areas to avoid and leaving scent trails to the best sources of food.

Get set

Let everyone know they will be worker ants foraging for food and building materials to take back to the nest. Like ants leaving a pheromone trail they will walk in a line, one behind the other. Remind the children that they should not pick up any rare or poisonous plants or any other dangerous items, such as broken glass. Encourage them to choose natural things.

Go!

Ants to the ready, head off foraging! As the ants walk off in a line, the first ant looks for something that attracts their attention. They pick it up and pass it down the line, each ant handing it to the ant behind. The first ant runs to the back, takes the object and holds on to it. Now the next ant in line at the front takes a turn. Keep going until all ants have gathered something. If the walk is long, the ants can each collect more than one object. Once the working ant party has finished foraging, take a look at the treasures that have been found for the colony! Each ant can talk about why they picked up what they did and possible benefits it has for the colony. Perhaps it's food for the ant larvae, or something to build the nest with, or a useful item such as a leaf boat, or it might just be something beautiful. The ants decide!

Endings

There's a lot to talk about when it comes to ants! These amazing creatures can nest almost anywhere, including next to water, up trees, underground and even in acorns. Their nests range from woven leaves, vast chambers with inbuilt air-conditioning to temporary bivouacs made from the linked legs of army ants. As seed dispersers and soil turners, they play a major role in the cycle of life. They can be extremely long lived for insects, with workers living for up to seven years and queens from 15 to 30 years.

Ants provide a great opportunity to talk about teamwork. What makes a good team? What skills are needed? This discussion can unfold in various ways and is always interesting. Ants are eusocial – they co-operate to take care of the young (rather than bring up offspring in individual families, as we do), and divide labour according to roles (ants have workers, soldiers and the egg-laying queen, for example). This system is quite rare. Other eusocial species include bees, wasps and termites. Interestingly, within vertebrates (the animal group that includes us) there are only two eusocial species: the naked mole rat and the Damaraland mole-rat.

Ask the children how they see ants now!

SLEEPING BEAR

Children are fascinated by bears, seeing them both as furry friends and as awesome forest beasts. They'll relish the chance to take on a bear's role, as well as the thrill of being an intruder, sneaking up on the bear and trying to steal its food! This game is all about tactics and using the senses to the full, so the various survival techniques adopted by different species add to the fun, whether the children decide to crawl low to the ground like a hunting cat or turn their heads like owls listening for prey. This game always generates a lot of laughter and the feeling of excitement is contagious.

Some children will be bursting to take a turn at being the bear or the intruder creeping up on it, while others may want to shy away from being the centre of attention. This game allows everyone to experience all these roles, with enthusiastic kids learning to wait and take turns in a fun environment, and the giggly, supportive team atmosphere encouraging the shyer ones to take part in whatever way they like. In other words, no one has to feel left out or 'less than'. This really boosts confidence, increasing a sense of self-worth.

Sleeping Bear is lively but doesn't need much open space so is perfect for playing under a tarp shelter on rainy days. It focuses the children's energy, brings them together as a group and opens the way for less physically active activities, such as craft, to follow.

Get ready

All the players link hands to make a circle, then spread out to make a bigger circle, before sitting down (let go before spreading out if there are not many of you). Choose someone to be the bear (everyone will get a turn eventually). The bear sits in the middle of the circle.

LOCATION	Any outdoor space
AGE GROUP	4 years +
NUMBER OF PLAYERS	8 +
LEARNING ABOUT...	Focus ۞ teamwork ۞ using senses ۞ tactical thinking ۞ self-esteem ۞ confidence ۞ connection to nature ۞ role play ۞ animal survival techniques ۞ empathy ۞ bears
KIT	→ Cotton scarf or other blindfold (optional) → Small item to represent the bear's food

Give the bear an object that will be its food. This can be something that bears actually eat, such as an apple or an acorn, or alternatively any item that's to hand, such as a hat or scarf that will represent food.

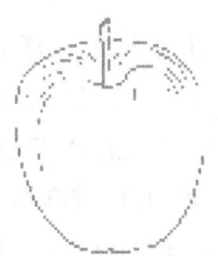

Get set

The bear puts the food next to them on the floor and then 'goes to sleep' – either you can blindfold it or it can simply close its eyes. Remind the bear, especially if it's not blindfolded, that peeking is not allowed! Also remind everyone in the circle to stay still and quiet so as not to confuse or wake the bear. When the sleeping bear is sitting quietly in the middle of the circle, the game leader points to someone in the circle. This is the intruder.

Go!

Intruder go! Try to get the food! As the intruder creeps up on the food, the bear has to listen carefully for the approaching intruder and try to reach out and touch them before the intruder steals the food. If the bear can do this, the bear has won this round of the game, and can choose to stay as the bear for the next round, or else return to the circle and pick someone else to be the bear.

If the person creeping up on the bear manages to get the food before the bear discovers them, they have won. Then they can become the bear, if they want to. If not, they can choose someone else to be the bear.

If a bear is particularly alert, choose two intruders and see if one of them can get the food.

Endings

Children love to learn facts about bears. You could talk about the eight species of bears around the world, from the black bear of North America to the polar bear, the largest bear, of the Arctic. It was once thought that bears in colder regions hibernated in winter, by going into a deep sleep (from which noise will not wake it) in order to conserve energy. It is now believed, however, that bears in colder regions den up in the winter and go into something called torpor, in which they sleep deeply to conserve energy. However, their body temperature remains relatively high, allowing them to wake up if disturbed. In this deep sleep brown and black bears, for example, can go without food, drink or passing waste for months, relying on muscle tissue and stored fats for water and energy. We humans are not capable of this amazing survival strategy.

> ### TRY THIS!
> **If someone you point to seems unsure, try to return to them later in the game. By now, with all the laughs and camaraderie, they may be willing to have a go.**

You could also discuss the different senses animals use to detect food or to protect themselves from scavengers and predators that might steal from them or try to eat them! A wolf's sense of smell, for example, is thought to be 100 times better than a human's – great for sniffing out food or scenting approaching threats. And the brown and unadorned greater wax moth *(Galleria mellonella)* may look somewhat dull but it has a brilliant skill for avoiding capture – its hearing is 150 times more sensitive than ours!

FURTHER READING

Bunney, Sarah, *The Illustrated Book of Herbs,* Octopus Publishing (London, 1984)

Cornell, Joseph, *Sharing Nature with Children,* Dawn Publications (California, 1998 Anv. edition)

Fearnley-Whittingstall, Hugh, *A Cook on the Wild Side,* Boxtree Ltd–Macmillan (London, 1997)

Garner, Lynne, *Little Book of Dens,* Featherstone Education–Bloomsbury Publishing (London, 2013)

Gill, Tim, *No Fear: Growing Up in a Risk Averse Society,* Calouste Gulbenkian Foundation (London, 2007)

Knight, Sara, *Forest School For All,* Sage Publications (London, 2011)

Louv, Richard, *Last Child in the Woods,* Workman Publishing (New York, 2005)

Philips, Roger, *Wild Flowers of Britain,* Pan Books (London, 1977)

Philips, Roger, *Wild Food,* Pan Books (London, 1983 8th edition)

Turner, JC and Van De Griend, P, *History and Science of Knots,* World

Scientific Publishing Co Ltd (London, 1996)

Find out more about Peter Houghton and Jane Worroll's Forest School at: www.playtheforestschoolway.com

ACKNOWLEDGMENTS

We want to thank:

Jane's mother, Maria Worroll-Meir, for her inspiring love of nature. Pete's family, for their creative influence and encouragement in pursuing interests in woodcraft.

Pete's Forest School trainer, Katharine, for sharing her passion for Forest School.

All our friends, for their practical help and support.

Jo Lal, for her belief.

Joseph Cornell, the Forest School pioneers, and all the outdoor centres (too many to mention here) that have paved the way to keep holistic learning in nature alive for children.

And our son, Theo, whose childlike exploration of the world reminds us to see things anew.

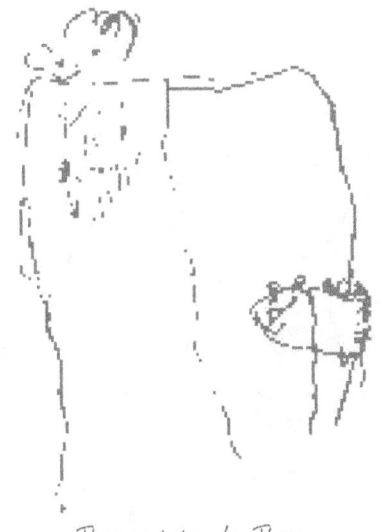

Theo and dog, by Theo

www.ingramcontent.com/pod-product-compliance
Lightning Source LLC
Chambersburg PA
CBHW050852230426
43667CB00012B/2251